Jay's Journey

JAY ROGERS

DEDICATION

Edmond Glen Utley
October 27, 1928 - November 27, 2007

This book is dedicated in loving memory of my great-granddaddy Edmond "Boat" Glen Utley. He was a great example and bright shining light to me and everyone who knew him.

> *"Ye are the light of the world. A city that is set on a hill cannot be hid. Neither do men light a candle, and put it under a bushel, but on a candlestick; and it giveth light unto all that are in the house. Let your light so shine before men, that they may see your good works, and glorify your Father which is in heaven."*
> *(Matthew 5:14-16)*

CONTENTS

ACKNOWLEDGEMENTS

How do I even begin to thank everyone who has contributed to my being the young man I am today? Words cannot even to begin to express my gratitude for all that has been done for me, but know these words are sincere.

First and foremost I must thank God for all the great blessings I have received in this life—there have been many. I give God the glory for getting me where I am today. With Him all things are possible (Philippians 4:13).

To Mom and Dad. Thank you for giving me the finest Christian home for which I could have asked. Thanks for loving me and straightening me out when I needed it most! Thanks for standing beside me and getting me through the past few years that have been so tough. I am who I am today because of what you both have taught me. I love you both very much and hope I have made you proud of the person I have become.

To Daniel. Thanks for trying to do everything in your power to encourage and cheer me up since I have been sick. Thanks for making me laugh during some of the most memorable and discouraging times in my life and for understanding when Mom and Dad had to be with me during some of your important milestones in your life. Thanks for always giving me a positive outlook. I love you. I could not have asked for a better brother and friend.

To my Aunt "Yane." Thanks for all the time you spent with me at home and in the hospital, and for helping Mom, Dad and Daniel out always, and without question when they needed it. Thanks for the scrap booking sessions (sorry I was such a slave driver), for the "back" scratches, all my food requests at the last minute, and for putting up with all my curious ways. I hope you had as much fun with me as I have with you. I love you!

To the rest of my family thank you for standing by me through thick and thin and for loving me, feeding me, entertaining me, and giving me something to laugh at. I love you.

To Derek. Man, what can I say? Not many people are fortunate enough to have a close friend their whole life like I have. You have been more of a brother than a friend. We made some of the greatest childhood memories and had some of the most memorable adventures that I will cherish for a lifetime. From the fish in your mom's bathtub to fighting over who was going tell my dad about the giant scratch in the new car, for the hot laps in your race car when I just knew I'd tear it up (fortunately I only drenched your helmet with sweat), for all the help with my school work, for sticking with me when I got sick and for simply sitting with me when I couldn't do anything because of the side effects of the chemo. I guess it kept us out of a lot of trouble. We sure could have tore up the town! I love you, man.

To Mr. Kelly and Momma 2. Thank you for making me part of your family and putting up with another mouth to feed. Sorry about the fish in the bathtub. It seemed like a good idea at the time. And besides, it was all Derek's idea! Jennifer, thanks for putting up with another "little brother." I love you all.

To the West Carroll Class of 2010, West Carroll Student body, and Jay's Warriors. Thank you for everything you have done for me throughout our high school years. The tributes and love you have shown me were very humbling. Thanks for not forgetting me even though I was unable to be at school much of the time. You always made me feel part of you. I wish you all the very best in your future.

To the faculty, staff and administration of West Carroll Special School District. Thanks for all your hard work and the times you went out of the way to help me with my greatest achievement to date—receiving my high school diploma! I couldn't have done it without you. You always went above and beyond. Also, thanks for being so good to my mom by letting her off work to be with me. It took a great burden off my family.

To the War Eagle football team. Thanks for your unwavering support. You all kept me going through some very hard times. You were the best team of which I ever had the privilege to be a part. I wish more than anything I could have been out on the field playing the game with you. Always be thankful you had the opportunity and ability to take the field on Friday nights.

To my coaches, Mr. Josh Fronabarger, Mr. Thomas Dees, and Mr. Chris Rich. Thank you for including me as a member of the team. I wish more than anything I could have been out on the field making you proud instead of standing on the sideline. Thanks for being such a positive influence on me and my teammates. I will always look back on those years as some of the greatest in my life. You all are the best!

To all my doctors at St. Jude and especially Dr. Lisa McGregor, Dr. Jessica Roberson, Dr. Matthew Krasin, and Dr. Trey Eubanks. Thank you for all the hard work you put into taking care of me! Without a doubt, I know you have given your all to help make me healthy. My family and I will forever be grateful for all the hard work and endless hours you have put in to make my, and many other lives, better. You all have been a blessing in our lives. I pray that one day you accomplish your goal; a cure for all with childhood cancer. Thank you for putting up with all my jokes, crazy stories, pictures of dead animals, and for working around my hunting schedule! I love you all.

A very special thank you to all my nurses at St. Jude. To my second floor nurses, thanks for putting up with me asking about "getting out" and threatening to escape every time you walked into my hospital room. Also, thanks for all the warm blankets and love you always gave me.

A very special thank you goes to Mrs. Julie Jones, Mrs. Pam Galliard, Mrs. Rachel Hester and all my D Clinic nurses. Thanks for going along with all my crazy stories, for making me laugh and for laughing with me. Thanks for straightening me out when I needed it and for comforting me when I was upset. You all keep me going! Also, thanks to Mrs. Kristie, the "front line" of D Clinic, for always having my counts ready for me when I showed up!

To Mrs. Sylvia Currie my medicine room nurse and friend. Thank you for always making me feel special, for all the gross surprises you dug out of the treasure box for me, for giving me a place to rest when I felt bad. Thanks for spoiling me rotten and for giving me a hug when I needed it, and for being there when I received my diploma. I love you, you're the very best.

To Mrs. Sarah Mann my BMT nurse. Thanks for taking the time just to talk to me when I was cooped up in the unit. You helped me laugh, smile, and pass the time. Thanks for taking such great care of me when I was your patient and for keeping up with me through my journey.

And last but not least, to Ms. Monica Daughtery, "Doctor Monica." Thanks for always making me laugh and keeping me straight! Someday I hope you become a "Survivor Fan." You really don't know what you are missing! You are a trip! Thanks for being my friend through the good and bad!

To my church families at Trezevant, Cades, Independence, and Pleasant Hill churches of Christ. Thank you for all your prayers, well wishes, friendship, meals, and support over the past several years. Isn't it wonderful to be a Christian!

To Mark Howell and Rachel Woolard. Thank you for all the hard work you put into my book. My dream of putting this book together could never have happened without your help.

To Mr. Kevin and Mrs. Sha Hill, Mr. Mike Tucker, May Processing and Taxidermy, Melvin Pittman, Odell Coleman, Benjie Lawrence, Jason McIntyre, Rob Bolton, Shane Steele, W&W Taxidermy, Catch-A-Dream Foundation, Cliff Covington, United Special Sportsman's Alliance, Jeremy Hage, Dave, Annette, and Mooney of Big Timber Hunts, Tennessee Extreme Outdoor Adventures, Mr. Steve Beilgard and family, and to all those who let me hunt on their land and brag about my kill. Thank you for giving me adventures of a lifetime! I enjoyed every minute of it and I will always cherish the memories you made possible for me. In my wildest dreams I never would have thought I would have been blessed enough to enjoy all these hunting experiences and trophies I have on my wall!

To all at Trenton Light and Water and The City of Trenton. Thank you for never failing to ask about me and how I was doing and for working with my dad concerning his job. Our family could not have made it without your generosity. Thank you to the TLW employees for the many meals you had waiting for me and my family when we returned home from our stays in the hospital. A very special thank you to Richy Turner and Ronald "Bom Bom" Williams for working so hard to pick up the slack on the job so my dad could be with me at my many trips to the doctor and stays in the hospital. You don't know what that gift has meant to me. Thanks for being his friend and seeing after him when Mom and I had to stay at St. Jude. It gave me comfort knowing that you were there for him while our family was separated.

To Mr. Mike Wetherington, Dwayne Culpepper, Tony Wyatt, ADC employees, TAUD employees, and all who contributed to my trip to the Alamo. You made my dream come true! I will forever be grateful you gave my family and me the opportunity to make those memories. Thank you.

My greatest apologies to all who have made this journey with me that I have failed to mention. Thank you to you all for your unwavering love and support you have so kindly shown me, and for continuing on the journey with me. I am truly blessed.

Thank you to all who have bought my book. I hope it both entertains and inspires you to persevere in times of trouble. Most of all, I hope it encourages you to have a closer walk with God.

With much Love,
Jay Rogers

Mom, Dad, Daniel, and me at the Alamo in San Antonio, Texas, 2010. Our trip was made possible through the generosity of TAUD, American Development Corporation and many, many other individuals and organizations.

1 Jay's Journey Begins

Who can remember all the way back to his own beginning? Certainly not me! So, who better could I call on for help with this chapter than the ones who were there—my Mom and Dad.

It all began on January 21, 1992 at Cape Fear Valley Hospital in Fayetteville, North Carolina. My Dad was serving in the United States Army and stationed at Fort Bragg. He served in Headquarters Company of the 27th Engineering Battalion, a combat engineering unit attached to the famed 82nd Airborne Division. He joined up during the first Gulf War but did not serve in combat. By the time his training was complete and he arrived at permanent party (Fort Bragg), the conflict was over. He was privileged to serve at the military memorial service of his unit's servicemen who gave the ultimate sacrifice for their country. I am so proud my dad had the desire to serve his country. I still love to listen to all his stories of his life in the military and his, as he would say, "jumping out of perfectly good airplanes."

I was brought home to a small single-wide trailer. It was located in Spring Lake, North Carolina, a suburb of Fayetteville. Evidently, when I came home I cried a whole lot, and was loud! All I wanted was to be held all the time—by only mom—and she says a lot of the time I still wasn't satisfied. It seems that all the crying was too much for Daniel, who at the time was two and a half years old and not fond of loud noises. He kept asking mom and dad if we could take me back to the doctor because I made too much noise. I guess he figured that's where I came from, and that if something was wrong with me, they, like Wal-Mart would exchange me for another one! When military housing on Ft. Bragg became available, we moved into a townhouse in the enlisted soldier's area. I was too young to remember much about that house, but from the pictures I have seen it looked really nice. It did not look anything like I would have imagined military housing to have looked.

After Dad's discharge from the U.S. Army, we moved close to his hometown of Trezevant. We rented a small house in Atwood, Tennessee just off U.S, Highway 79, only four miles down the road from Trezevant. We lived there for a couple years until the company for which Dad worked sent us north to Iowa City, Iowa. After several months, that company wanted to give him a promotion. That was good! But, they wanted to send him to either California or Chicago. Neither Mom nor Dad wanted Daniel and me to grow up in the city, so we headed back south.

We stopped first in Memphis, Tennessee. We are by no means city folks, nor did we have any desire to live in the city, but that was where Dad found a job. He said he took the job in Memphis because the company said they would have an opening closer to Trezevant in a few months. While in Memphis, we stayed with my aunt and her family for a few weeks. Two families in one house? Not a good idea! Way too crowded!

While Dad was still working in the city, he and Mom found, and bought, a small house just outside Trezevant. It was across the street from the Rogers' family farm. In times past, many members of the Rogers-Pinson family had lived on Oak Grove road where our house was located. Now, most have either passed on or moved away, but much of the land still belongs to their descendants. Our house had previously belonged to members of my dad's family. And so, we were finally "home"! Though Dad still worked in Memphis, he came home on the weekends. A few months after we bought that house, Dad did get transferred back to the Jackson, Tennessee area and was able to be home with Mom, Daniel, and me all the time.

We sold that house a couple years later and bought my Grandaddy J.L and Grandmamma Frances' house which was across the street and down the road a ways. I was around 4 years old at the time we moved into the Rogers' house. It was at this location on Oak Grove Road just outside Trezevant that most of my own childhood memories began.

I have many great memories of the years we lived on the farm. A few of those memories stand out in my mind that I would like to share. Including our land and the land belonging to my aunt Millie Burke, I had 70 acres on which to roam. Through the years my brother Daniel and I had dirt bikes and four wheelers we drove all through the woods and trails that crisscrossed our land and the land that surrounded us. Our farm had mostly row crops and when the crops were out I loved to take off across the field wide open on my four wheeler. Mom eventually found out and put a stop to that. She told me one time she saw me standing up instead of sitting on the seat, flying across the field and hollering. It's a wonder I didn't wreck and hurt myself badly. It wasn't long after she caught me that the four wheelers were sold.

Back when paintball guns started getting big, I guess I was around eight or nine years of age, maybe younger, Dad, Daniel, and I joined that craze. We bought three really nice guns, but as for safety equipment—it never even crossed our minds! One day we decided we were going to play paintball war. Daniel and I were going to be a team and Dad and Rex, our chocolate lab, would be a team. We decided Daniel and I would hide first and that Dad and Rex would come and find us. Of course, the last one not hit with a paint ball would be the winner. Daniel and I took off through the fields to the back pond lot. It was wooded around it and we had a lot of spots to hide. Oh, and it was winter so there were no snakes, ticks, or chiggers out (for those of you who were wondering about that). We just knew we had the perfect place to hide. Our plan was to stay hidden until Dad got close enough, and then let loose on him with our paintball guns. We knew victory was ours for the taking! We were hidden and being pin drop quiet. Next thing we knew, Rex came running to the thicket behind which we were hiding! What in the world! We kept telling Rex to go away but he kept making noise and Dad found out where we were hiding! He hollered out to us but Daniel said to stay quiet and we would get him when he got closer! I was always easily spooked by things, and for some reason I just couldn't stand the thought of being pummeled by those paintballs because they do hurt. So, in my infinite wisdom, I shot out all my paintballs in the air and since I was out of ammunition I hollered, "cease fire Daddy, cease fire." The game was over, Dad won and Daniel was so mad he could have burst!

That was not the first time, nor was it the last time Daniel and I did not see eye to eye. It seems we went through a phase where we were having a hard time getting along. I have been told it is nothing out of the ordinary for brothers not to always get along. During one of our fights my dad had gotten a belly full of hearing us argue. He came up with an "activity" that would force us to work together to get it done. Dad gave us two shovels and a wheel barrow and sent us to the drainage ditch behind the house. We were to work together to get it cleaned out. It was nasty and it stank. While we were cleaning out that mucky ditch, Daniel and I seemed to get madder and madder at each other—until we discovered several turtles buried in it. We ended up having a pretty good time in that ditch in spite of the fact that we got covered in mud and rotten leaves and left it smelling like we had been playing in the sewer. I don't remember that little lesson giving us a new appreciation for each other, but now that we are grown, we are much better friends and look back on that punishment and laugh.

I was fortunate enough to attend school in the same district (West Carroll) from kindergarten through graduation. That allowed me to grow up with the same group of friends. However, one in particular stood out and we became good friends. In first grade I started taking up with a kid by the name of Derek Box. We just kind of stuck with one another. We were both mischievous and seemed to like a lot of the same things, so we hit it off pretty good. From then on, we were always the best of friends. People used to ask us if we were brothers. Both our families always answered, "Yes." I guess it was because we were always together and from a distance it was hard to tell who was who. We were about the same height, same build, and we both had light brown hair that turned blonde from the summer sun. After a while, Derek's mom claimed me and my mom claimed him as her own. Needless to say, we generally stayed into something all the time, some of it good and some not so good.

Whether Derek and I were at his house or mine, we always had our bicycles. We lived close enough to each other that we were able to ride back and forth between our houses. The worst part about the trip was having to ride past the dogs at Ms. Jean Autry's house Every time we rode past, without fail, a pack of dogs would chase us like we were steak on wheels!

One place my mom and dad told us to never ride our bicycles was under our carport alongside our car. They were afraid we would scratch the car—our new car. Like most kids, we didn't listen to what we were told. One day in particular we decided to disobey those orders and ride our bikes under the carport anyway. We thought we needed to park them in front of the car while we went in the house. While riding past the car, Derek's handlebar scraped against it. I could tell by just the sound that was made that we were about to be in big trouble. His handlebar grips were on the bike, but unfortunately the ends were worn off from all the times we just threw them down instead of using the kickstands. Yep, you guessed it! He gouged a line about six inches long all the way down to the metal. Talk about panicking, we were! We spent the whole afternoon fighting about who was going to tell Dad the new car was scratched up. We almost came to blows over that one! When Dad got home we finally decided to tell him and Mom what had happened. We were both scared to death and bawling like a couple of babies! We took our tongue thrashing and came out on the other side okay. We never did ride our bikes under the carport again! Lesson learned!

As boys usually do, we enjoyed being outdoors. We spent a lot of time fishing. Derek's aunt had a pond that had all kinds of fish in it. One summer day we decided to head over to her place and try to catch a few fish. After having great success, we came home with a lunchbox full of bream. Yep, a lunchbox—we crammed them in it. I can't believe they made it all the way back to Derek's house alive. I don't really remember what we planned to do with them but we knew we couldn't keep all those fish alive in the lunchbox for long. So, we decided that the only thing we had that was big enough to hold them all was Derek's mom's bathtub. You read it right, the bathtub. We ran cold water and filled it as full as it would get. We then dumped the lunchbox full of fish into the tub. They seemed to like it; at least they swam around in it. We didn't get in too much trouble; Mrs. Rita fussed but couldn't help but laugh. I still do too every time I look back on it.

Most hot summer days Derek and I would spend at his house because he had a swimming pool. We would swim and eat, eat and swim. One of our favorite snacks was the *Chicken in a Biskit™* crackers. There is no telling how many boxes we put away in a week. It was several, I know. At one point, in all this eating and swimming and swimming and eating we started to get lazy. We no longer separated the two activities but combined them—we ate while we swam. There wasn't really any swimming going on. We just stayed in the pool while we ate. You know what? You don't really get cramps from getting in a pool too soon after you eat. Out of all the times we ate in the pool we never once got a cramp or ever got sick. Myth busted! Derek and I have remained close all these years and graduated together with the West Carroll High School Class of 2010. God has blessed me with a friend that I consider a brother.

As I mentioned before, we lived on the family farm. In 1996 my aunt and her family moved back to Trezevant, and for a while lived in Boat's (my grandfather Glen Utley's) trailer until they could find a house. It was then that Daniel and I started spending quite a lot of time with our cousins: Haley, Zack, and Logan Chrisman. They later moved uptown and then back to the farm, right next door to our house. We all got into quite a bit there on the farm. Most of the time we got along pretty well, but sometimes we would get on each other's nerves and end up in a fight. I remember one time in particular Daniel, Zack, Logan, and I were playing outside in our backyard. Logan, being several years younger than the rest of us, tended to get on all our nerves. It seems like he was forever carrying on with some nonsense that would aggravate us so one day we decided to teach him a lesson. We picked him up, hooked his britches on the support to Mom's clothesline and went off and left him. He let loose hollering like a skinned cat. We thought it was hilarious. The next time he would think twice about annoying us! I believe Haley heard him hollering and went and got him down. We may not have always gotten along, but being family we always forgave each other—most of the time!

My cousins on my mom's side are quite a bit younger than Daniel and me. As I write this chapter, Dylan is in fourth grade and Lily is in first grade. They live in Medon, Tennessee, just south of Jackson. They are not next door, but are close enough for us to see them often. Since my mom's parents lived in Trezevant, my aunt would often come to stay with them and bring Lily and Dylan over to the house to stay with us. One day while we were outside on the trampoline, Dylan and I decided we wanted to swim; the only problem was we didn't have a swimming pool. We searched around the farm for something we could use to swim in and the only thing we found that would hold water was a fifty-five gallon drum. We filled it up and climbed inside. We called it our "redneck swimming pool." It really didn't make much of a pool though. We only stayed in it long enough for Mom to make our picture. That photo is one of my Mom's favorites.

We lived there for 13 years until my dad's work took us to Trenton, Tennessee in 2006. We built a house near the Gibson County Lake. This is where we currently live, and I just love it out here. Mom and Dad bought seven acres with an acre and a half pond that is full of bass, bream, and catfish. Ironically, I don't spend much time fishing now unless someone is visiting and they want to go. But, the great thing about the pond is that it attracts deer and other thirsty wildlife. I've been very tempted to shoot at them out the door!

Looking back over my childhood I have been reminded how God has blessed me with such a wonderful family. Not everyone is fortunate enough to have the kind of home and raising I have had. Mom and Dad always gave Daniel and me unconditional love. They created traditions and moments that I look back on with the fondest of memories. But most importantly, they taught us the importance of being obedient to God. Grandparent's houses were and still are a special place to go. Aunts and uncles houses are an extension of home and my cousins are friends. My family has always been my greatest source of strength and support throughout my childhood. I could not imagine any of it being any better.

2 Jay's Journey With Boat

Boat? Who is *Boat*?

That's what everyone asks when I talk about Boat, my great grandfather, Glen Utley. Why did I call him Boat, you ask? It's like this, Boat got his name long before I came into the world. Actually my older brother, Daniel, gave him the name. When Daniel was about a year and a half old, he, Mom, and Dad lived in middle Tennessee. They would occasionally come home to Trezevant to visit. Daniel was the first, and at the time, the only grandchild, so needless to say he was a little spoiled. Aunts, uncles, and especially grandparents usually did what Daniel wanted them to do. Boat was no exception. It seemed that whatever any of his great grandchildren wanted to do, Boat was up for the challenge. That tradition began with Daniel and had the trickle-down effect with the rest of us.

Daniel loved to walk and explore things. He was especially fascinated with the outdoors. Boat would take Daniel outside and spend hours following him around the farm. They had all the out buildings they had to visit—the well house, the tractor shed, and the barn. Their tour would begin and end with the tractor shed with lots of other rabbits having been chased in between. It was what was in the tractor shed that made that building so special. At the time, there was a big boat stored in it. It was called the "tractor shed," but the boat overshadowed the tractor and all the other machinery stored inside.

Daniel was mesmerized by the boat. He had just started talking and Mom and Dad said they guessed that "Granddaddy" was a bigger mouthful for him to say than "Boat." Every time he saw Granddaddy, no matter where they were, he would go to him, hold his hands up to Granddaddy (wanting to be picked up) and say "Boat"! From that point on, Granddaddy Glen was called "Boat."

A few years later, when I was a couple years old, we bought my great Granddaddy and Grandmama Rogers' house on the family farm in Trezevant. It just happened to be next door to Boat's house. For as far back as I remember, many of my memories include the time Boat and I spent together and the many projects with which we tinkered.

My memories are filled with the hours Boat and I spent in his shed working with wood. He rarely threw anything away for fear he might be able to use it in the future. He always kept scrap wood because scrap pieces were perfect for building bird houses. One of my favorite projects was building bluebird houses for my mom. Boat knew all about bluebirds and what kind of houses they liked to live in. He knew the exact size of the hole needed for them to get in and out of the house. He said that if we cut a bigger hole than what the bluebird needed, larger birds would keep the bluebirds out and use it to build their own nests. Boat said bluebirds don't like messy houses either, so we would have to build them so one side of the house would swing open so Mom could clean out the old nests from year to year. Still today, Mom has those houses up on fence posts around the edge of our property. The houses have the hinges so they can be opened up but she's not very good at keeping them cleaned out.

Boat and I also made wooden keepsake boxes and paddles. The only problem was the paddles were not the kind with which you rowed a boat. I had to talk Boat out of making any more of those because they sure did sting when Mom used them on my backside! (I was a hard-headed kid.) I still have most of the boxes we made. They mean a lot to me because they bring back so many good memories of the time we spent together and all the different things he taught me.

Sometimes when Boat and I felt like being lazy, or when he started having health problems and feeling bad and was not able to work as hard or as long anymore, we would sit under the elm tree he had planted and swing in the swing. We made lots of plans underneath the shade of that tree. Some of those plans were accomplished and some were not. But, it sure was a lot of fun making those plans just the same. That swing has long ago been taken down, and the elm tree has since died and I sure do miss the swing, the tree, and the good times I had there.

When the seasons changed and cold weather came around, Boat and I spent our time in the house "piddling." Boat collected coins which was very fascinating to me. I liked to spend time going through his collection and listening to the stories of how he came upon a particular coin or what it reminded him of. Boat always had a story about the coins and could tell me a lot about them. He used the wood keepsake boxes we made in which to keep his collection. The part of his coin collection that fascinated me the most was not the rarest, or oldest, or the most valuable. It was a giant glass container, about the size of an old milk can, filled with pennies. It was so heavy he had to move it by dragging it on a piece of carpet. It was entirely too heavy to pick up , but of course I had to try. He was afraid the bottom of the glass container would burst. After Boat died Granny and Papaw (Glenda Utley Rogers and J.T. Rogers) took that container to the bank for all those pennies to be counted. Boy did those ladies at the bank have a fit over that! I had always wondered how much those pennies would add up to be. I believe it came out to around $70.

Boat's house was also my favorite after school destination. Every day, Daniel and I would ride the school bus so we could beat Mom home. She worked at school and always got home about twenty minutes after we got off the bus. We rarely went to our house, instead we always went down to Boat and Mamaw's house. If we went straight home, Mom would always find something for us to do like take the garbage out or feed the dog before we started our homework. If we went to Boat's house first, we got to relax and eat before starting on our chores and homework. One day while I was away at school, Boat made me a little desk. I was so excited! With it I could sit in his living room in front of the TV, do my homework and eat my snack.

I always had a snack when I went to Boat and Mamaw's house. They always had the best snacks! I remember one time in particular that Mamaw took me to the local grocery store. She followed me around with a buggy and let me buy whatever I wanted. Boat and I had a bunch of snacks that day! One of Boat's and my favorite snacks was milk and cornbread. Each of us would get a coffee mug or a small bowl and crumble up warm, fresh-baked cornbread Mamaw had just taken out of the oven. We would fill that mug just about up to the top then pour milk over it. Buttermilk for Boat and sweet milk for me. I wanted to fix mine like Boat's but that buttermilk was too thick, and besides it looked and tasted ruined. Sweet milk and bread tasted just fine to me! I still have milk and bread for a snack sometimes, but it is not as good as what I fixed at Boat and Mamaw's house.

Another of our favorite snacks was *Little Debbie®* *Oatmeal Crème Pies*. Boat always had them in the house and if he didn't and we decided we wanted a pie for our snack, we would load up in the car and head to town to get some. Later, when I got older and Boat got sick, we would have to pick up groceries at the store for him. I never let Mom and Dad forget to get him his oatmeal pies.

Sometimes while eating our snack we would decide to watch a little television. Boat never had cable or satellite so we watched what he could pick up with the tower antenna. One of our favorite after school shows was "Clifford The Big Red Dog." It came on PBS, and was always one channel that regardless of what the weather was doing it would come in pretty good. I always thought that Boat enjoyed it as much as I did. Truth be told, I was probably a little too old for it myself, but we enjoyed it all the same. It was not the show, it was the company that made it worth watching. After Clifford, there wasn't anything else on so Boat would turn over to channel seven and wait for the evening news to come on. The "Maury Povich" show was usually on at that time. We never did pay much attention to it but sometimes it got rough enough it would make us notice what was going on and Boat would turn it off. I can remember him saying "That ain't fit to watch." Sometime later Boat got a VCR and when "Clifford" was over we would put in a movie. We didn't have to mess with "Maury" anymore.

I mentioned earlier that Boat was sick. He was diagnosed with Parkinson's Disease several years before he passed away. As the disease progressed, he needed the assistance of a wheelchair to get around the house. My Dad and Papaw built a ramp onto his deck so he was able to get outside. It was the neatest wheelchair I had ever seen. It was bright red, motorized, and I had the biggest time riding in it—all the great-grandkids did. Boat lived in a mobile home, so needless to say there was not a lot of room to maneuver the wheelchair. When he would ride it back into his bedroom, he would sometimes have a hard time getting it turned so he could come back out. Since my hand was steadier than his, he would have me drive it out of the bedroom and through the hallway. More times than not, it took a detour out the door before I made it back to the living room. Boat's driveway was gravel but it was packed hard, and was long, and smooth. I would crank up the speed on the wheelchair and go up and down the driveway so fast that I would kick up a dust cloud behind me. Often, when my friend Derek Box came over, that was one of the things we would do.

At that time, I would never have imagined that just a few years in the future I would have a need for a wheelchair similar to Boat's. I have trouble walking long distances and up and down hills. It causes my legs to hurt and I tire easily so my doctor wrote a prescription so I could have a motorized wheelchair to help me get around outside the house. I'm so proud I have it so I can continue to enjoy my normal activities. I look at it this way—at least I had lots of practice on Boat's chair, so I have no trouble operating mine!

One of the hardest days of my life was when Boat was no longer able to stay at home. His health had declined to the point he was no longer able to stay by himself and we were no longer able to give him the care he needed at home. I was lost without Boat next door. I missed my friend. The only time I was able to see him was when someone would take me to the rest home. Granny got to where she would wait to visit him until school was out in the afternoon so I was able to go with her. We would stop at the store or restaurant to pick up things he needed or some of his favorite foods he liked to eat. I loved walking in and seeing the smile on his face when we showed up. I can remember thinking to myself how I couldn't wait till I got my driver's license so I could go see Boat whenever I wanted and did not have to depend on getting a ride with someone. Unfortunately that day never came. By the time I had gotten my driver's license I was taking chemotherapy. One of the side effects of chemo is low counts. What I mean by that is my body's ability to fight infection and sickness was extremely low and at times non-existent. Because of my compromised immune system, I was not able to see Boat as often as I would have liked. Boat and I wanted to see each other so badly. I can remember walking around the outside of the nursing home and going to Boat's window. We tried to visit through the glass and would even talk over the phone so he could hear me better. I can remember telling him goodbye through the glass and both of us crying—me because I missed him so but was unable to be with him, and he because he was so upset because I was sick and going through so much. Boat was always so tenderhearted. He never could stand seeing his family hurt or upset. I remember though, that Boat never did complain about his illness or having to leave his house and go live at the nursing home. He was always kind to everyone he came across and always put other's needs before his own. He saw after us all as long as he was able and he was always obedient to God. Someday I know I will see him again, not because I'm perfect but because, like Boat, I have always tried my best to be obedient to God.

3 Jay's Journey With Sports

If it has a ball that's hit, chased, or thrown, if it has a finish line, or if points are scored, chances are I've played it or at least watch it. It is an understatement to say that I am an avid sports fan. I follow some sports more closely than others. I have also enjoyed playing sports—some more than others.

I began my journey into the wide world of sports at the young age of four. The first trying of my skill was at Tee Ball. I was on the West Carroll Primary PTO sponsored team. It was one of the few times I was a member of a team of which my dad wasn't my coach. My coach that year was Mr. Ron Cox who lived in McLemoresville, Tennessee. I started out as one of the smallest players on the team but I could hit the ball as well, and in some cases, better than those who were a lot bigger than me. I really tried hard to do my best and always received encouragement from Mom and Dad. One way they encouraged me was cheering me on with a few words when I was up to bat or chasing a ball.

Most of the time they would say my name followed by the word "son," as in, "Jay, son, run faster" or Jay, son, catch the ball." I guess Mr. Ron thought my name was "Jason," because that is what he called me. I finally asked Mom and Dad why the coach kept calling me "Jason." Finally, after seeing how badly it bothered me, Dad had to tell Mr. Ron that my name was Jay.

After that season Dad began coaching my baseball team. By that time, I had grown quite a bit and was now bigger than most of my teammates. Along with my growth came the ability to hit the ball even better. The following year, I moved up to "player pitch" and was on the Tigers team. I didn't have to be drafted because Dad was the coach and so I would obviously play on his team. That year, I had a hard time hitting the ball. I guess my coordination wasn't the best. It was a little disappointing to me since the previous year I had been able to really hit the ball. I think a lot of the kids had the same problem because the following year the league changed things up a little and made my age group go to "machine pitch."

The season we started using the pitching machine was my favorite year of playing baseball. The name of my team was the Cubs. I was lucky enough to have a lot of my close friends on the same team so that made going to the ball field almost every night even more fun. Also, my hitting greatly improved (and so did everyone else's). Going to machine pitch was the right thing to do. It was also that year that I began playing in the catcher's position. I really loved that because I was always in the middle of the action. By then I was big enough that people thought twice about trying to run over me!

After my last year of machine pitch, I moved up to join a team called the Yankees. I was excited about moving up, but the name of the team left a little to be desired. I have never been much of a Yankees fan. In fact, I can't stand the Yankees—the New York ones! Dad and Mr. Greg McClain were my coaches, so I knew it would be a fun year. That was the only year that Daniel, my brother, and I were able to play baseball on the same team. That year I began playing third base instead of catcher. Cody Nelson got to play catcher. He was tall and skinny and could move a lot faster than me—I was a chunk. I was a little upset at first, but in the end I enjoyed playing third base more than playing catcher.

During my first year with the Yankees my hitting suffered again. I was now playing with the "big boys" and they pitched really fast—a lot faster than what I was used to! All of us who had moved up to the older age group struggled some. I tried, I really did, but I couldn't hit that ball for anything. The only way I got on base was to either get walked or crowd the plate and take the hit from the ball. Often, I took one for the team!

Later in the season I came to the conclusion that getting hit by the ball sure was getting painful. Add to that the fact that by that time many of the pitchers knew I wouldn't swing and were themselves getting more accurate. I was getting struck out more than not. My strategy had to change so I began swinging at the high balls that came across the plate. It drove Mr. Greg nuts! He told me every time I was up to bat: "Lay off the high ones." One specific time I remember being at bat and the ball being thrown high—my favorite! I swung and hit it, knocking it straight over the third baseman's head. It landed in left field and I was in business! I ended up getting on third base, where Mr. Greg was the base coach. After the play was finished, and while we were waiting for the next batter to come to the plate, I turned to talk to Mr. Greg and the first thing he said was, yep, you guessed it: "Lay off the high ones!"

The older I got the less interest I had in baseball. The same was true for my friend Derek Box. From the time we were real young we had spent our summers playing ball. Derek and I could never make the decision when we were going to quit, so we made an agreement that when we did quit we would quit at the same time. I guess we would never commit because that was all we ever did with our summers—playing ball and hanging out with our friends. Every year we would always have to make the decision as to whether we would play or not. One year I guess we gave each other the wrong impression—he signed up, and I didn't. When it came time for practices to begin we discovered what had happened. There were no hard feelings but we still argue and joke about it to this day. The following year we *both* retired from baseball.

Though my baseball career was "officially" over I did make a brief comeback. My brother Daniel continued to play. He was in the Babe Ruth league, the big league! It was the oldest boy's league in summer baseball going up to nineteen years old. The name of his team was MADCO. His coaches were Dad and Mr. Jeff Palmer, owner of MADCO, the company that sponsored our team. Sometimes having all the players show up for a game was a bit of a challenge. Some of the them had part time jobs, summer family vacations and other teenage distractions. Most of the time this wasn't a problem except for one game I so easily remember. MADCO was short one player and in my infinite wisdom, I volunteered to fill the empty spot. With the team now complete it was time to play ball. The first time I got up to bat I didn't dare crowd the plate as I was so famously known to do. Those boys were big and could throw twice as hard as any pitcher I had ever been up against. I was not about to "take one for the team" at this level! I was even able to resist "the high ones" that I always like so well. I didn't even swing! I just stood there and let the balls fly by. That happened each time I was up to bat. The thing about it was the other team's pitcher never did get the clue that I had no intention of even trying to swing at the ball and they walked me every time. My Babe Ruth batting record was zero strikeouts, zero home runs and two times on base. Two walks but I'll take it! After that game I returned to retirement and never did play baseball again, but I can't say I missed it. I was on to bigger and better things.

In 2004, while in the seventh grade, I began trapshooting. The 4-H organization in Carroll County, Tennessee began forming trapshooting teams from school students from all over Carroll County. My dad received a call one evening from Mr. Roger McAlexander. He was working with Mr. Kenny Herndon from the 4-H program to form junior and senior level teams with students from West Carroll, Huntingdon, and Clarksburg schools.

We had knew Mr. Roger from football. His son, Alex and my brother Daniel had played football together all the way from the Pee Wee league through high school. Mr. Roger knew that I was a big hunter and thought that I might be interested in joining the team. When Dad told me about it, I thought it would be a good fit, so I told him to count me in. I was asked to talk to my friends at school to see if anyone else would be interested in shooting. I asked several people and several tried it but only one of my friends, Colby Cooper, and I decided to try out for the team. We tried out for the junior squad and both Colby and I made it. We were the only members of the Carroll County Claybusters Junior squad that were from West Carroll. There were others from West Carroll that shot on the senior squad.

Our season started later than most teams. We only had three months to shoot before the State trapshooting tournament. The teams were formed from shooting averages of how many clay pigeons you hit for the first few weeks of the shooting season. When the teams were put together, Colby and I had made the number one junior team. The first team had five shooters and two reserves which were the members with the highest shooting averages from the second Carroll County Claybusters team. The members of the first team were Justin Baker, first shooter from Huntingdon, Heath Bartholomew, second shooter from Clarksburg, Colby Cooper, third shooter from West

Carroll, me, fourth shooter also from West Carroll and Jacob Allen, fifth shooter from Huntingdon.

Our home shooting range was E.V's Southgate Gun Club in Lavinia, Tennessee. We would usually practice every Thursday afternoon. Each shooting range has five positions facing an open field with the trap machine about twenty feet or so in front of the concrete shooting positions. We would begin in our shooting position of which mine was fourth. You would rotate after shooting twenty five shells until you shot in each of the five positions. We completed this rotation four times each practice. In order to qualify for the state tournaments you were required to shoot a certain number of rounds. We had to work fast. After a lot of work and mountains of shotgun shells we made it to the Tennessee State Tournaments. After two days of shooting we tied for fourth place with a team from McKenzie, Tennessee. It came down to a shoot off which ended up with our team winning the shoot off. If I remember correctly, we beat them by one target. Out of nearly seventy teams in the state of Tennessee we ended up in fourth place. We were quite happy we had done so well. We had not been shooting together nearly as long as the other teams we competed against but still we won. We returned home, very proud of our achievement and with a ticket to the Grand Nationals in Vandalia, Ohio.

At the Grand Nationals, the top five teams from each state tournament as well as the top teams from other countries earned a spot to compete for the top spot in the world of Shooting Sports. We arrived just weeks after the State tournament in Vandalia which was hosting the Grand for the last time. It had been nearly one hundred years since the first Grand National had been hosted in that city. The following year the tournament would be moved to a new facility in Illinois.

We arrived at the Grand in late July with the beginning of the school year just days away. Our first day in Vandalia consisted of practice and shopping the different vendor booths that were set up on the strip. That evening we returned to the hotel after going out for supper and had a great time swimming in the pool and goofing off. The following day began with the real deal—the Grand National Tournament, the "Super Bowl" of shooting sports. We started early in the morning and it was already unbearably hot. We shot well throughout the day moving up in the standings earning us a spot in day two of the tournament. With the conclusion of day two, final standings were posted and we took eighteenth place. I don't remember the exact amount of teams entered in the tournament but it was hundreds. I thought we did really well for just a bunch of boys from Carroll County who were thrown together just three months earlier.

Even though the tournament was over and we were headed home we couldn't wait till the next year. Can you imagine how good we would be after a year of practice? We intended to return to the Grand and win! Though I did not know it at the time, that was to be the last time I would shoot in competition. In November of 2005 my illness required that I undergo surgery to remove the top two ribs from my right side. My shoulder could no longer take the repeated kick of the gun from the hundreds of rounds I would have to shoot. I am still able to shoot a gun when hunting but unfortunately, I have been unable to continue competing.

Thinking back, I guess I would have to say that football was my all time favorite sport. When I was just a little bitty fellow I would tell Mom and Dad that someday I was going to play college and then professional football. Back then they got really tickled because I would tell them I was either going to play college ball at the University of Tennessee or Bethel a small local college in McKenzie, Tennessee. At that time, I was "undecided" as to where I really wanted to go. After my college career I intended to find a home on the best football team in the NFL—the Tennessee Titans. Well at least that was my dream!

My football career began a little something like this. At the age of four I started playing flag football in the West Carroll Pee Wee football league. I was drafted to the Seminoles team and we had a less than good record that season, but we had a lot of fun. The following year I became a War Eagle because my dad began coaching that team along with Mr. Greg McClain. I played the positions of center on offense and defensive tackle on defense. We had a really good team and most of the time fought for the number one spot against the Vols team. They had the speed and we had the size. My good friend, Derek, was on the Vols team and so we were not able to be teammates until we moved up to the junior tackle league.

One of the favorite plays my team had was called the "sitting duck." It was a trick play that took the other teams a couple years to figure out. That play was the one we would use when we were in desperate need of a first down. It confused the other team so much that it almost always resulted in a touchdown. I was the center, after the ball was hiked the quarterback, (who if I remember correctly was Hayden McClain) would touch the ball and fake a hand off to our running back, Brandon French. While all this was taking place I was still in stance holding on to the ball. With the attention elsewhere, the tight end, Cody Nelson would come around from behind the opposite way from which Brandon came from and would grab the ball and head for the end zone!

The year I was in second grade my brother played in the older boys league, the Junior Tackle league. As I mentioned earlier I was one of the bigger boys on the flag team, and being that my dad was one of the coaches of Daniel's team, the Steelers, I was allowed to suit up and practice with them. I was stout and hardheaded enough that I gave them all a run for their money. I loved the tackle game and could not wait till the next year to move up and play in that league. When that time did come, I was put on the Chiefs team. Daniel had moved up to play Junior High ball with West Carroll and Dad became one of the Chiefs coaches along with Mr. Greg McClain. Though I had practiced with the Steelers team it didn't hurt my feelings any that I was not playing for them because I've never been much of a Steelers fan! I was glad to be on the Chiefs team. Mr. Greg had previously been my coach for baseball and I had played ball with his boys, Clint and Hayden. As it happened Derek Box also got drafted to play with the

Chiefs. At this time Derek and I were the same height and size, we also had the same hair color. People would say we looked like twins out on the field. Those who did not know us thought we were brothers. Even our moms had trouble telling us apart from a distance. Since we were the same size we were partnered up for practice drills. It sure was bad to have to hit hard against your friend. We were on the same team through our years in junior tackle and never had to play against each other and really hit each other hard. During my time on the Chiefs team, I played the same positions I had played in flag football.

The last year I spent in junior tackle the Pee Wee league came up with an All-Star team. It was made up of the best players from the five junior tackle teams. We played teams from other area towns. We ended up having a great season. Our defense never allowed a team to score against us. The closest anyone came to scoring was our last game against McKenzie when they got in our Red Zone (within the twenty yard line). Our defense huddled up and got so fired up that when the play was put in motion they were stopped dead in their tracks!

After several years on the junior tackle squad it was time to move up and play Junior High ball for West Carroll. It was one of two moments I had been waiting for—the second moment being when I moved up to the High School team. I joined the junior high squad and earned a place on the starting lineup. I was again on the line playing the same positions I had in the past—center and nose guard. I was so excited when I made first string. When we were given our jerseys, I was number 67 and Derek was number 68. Our coach was Mr. Josh Fronabarger; he would later move up and be our coach on the high school team. He also gave me a nickname by which some of my nurses would later called me. Coach Fronabarger gave me the nickname "Skillet" after Daniel knocked an iron skillet off one of the beams in my Granny's kitchen. It ended up hitting me in the middle of my forehead giving me a big bruise and knot right in plain sight. The next day in practice I had trouble getting my football helmet on and off. But I sure wasn't going to miss practice over not being able to get my helmet on. Missing practice would keep me out of the game that coming Thursday. While on the practice field, coach called me over to him and told me to take off my helmet so he could see my head. For a while after that I was known as "Skillet." I ended up taking the tape off my helmet that had my name on it and replacing it with a piece that had "Skillet" written on it.

In my first year at West Carroll Junior High, we started our season with a 5-0 record. We had a really good season. The last game was slated to be against Huntingdon. The winner would be the Carroll County champs. We wanted this one really bad. There was no trophy or anything for the winner—it was just the pride that came with being the best Junior High team in the county. Though we played our hearts out, the game ended with the score being 20-22, in Huntingdon's favor.

After what we thought was the last game of the season, we had an additional game added to our schedule. It was to be an All-Star game. Our team was going to go up against the best from Gibson County. Most were from Medina and Dyer with a few from other Gibson County schools. Again we played a tough game with the All Star team squeaking by us 14-12. Our record that year ended up being 5-2.

For my eighth grade year we had a new coach, Mr. Mark Rich. He was the cousin of the High School head football coach Mr. Chris Rich. Coach Fronabarger had moved up to help with the high school team. We missed him a lot but we all liked our new coach. He was like a big kid and fit in with us really well. We had a good season that year but as it was drawing to an end I began having trouble with injuries. First, I had trouble with a sprained ankle and my shoulder hurting but I was determined not to let that keep me from playing, so I pressed on ignoring the pain. Our last game came around and once again it was with Huntingdon. The night of that game, my shoulder was hurting worse than it ever had before. I had been to the doctor and he thought it was probably a separation in the shoulder. After a game it would hurt and then get better until after the next game. I was determined to finish the season even if I had to suffer through the pain to play because I did not want to let my teammates down. And of course, this last game was against Huntingdon and there was no way was I missing this one—my team needed me!

Dad told me not to play if I was hurting, people would understand. But we were so close to winning. It was just like last year we were neck and neck. It was the last minutes of the fourth quarter, we were ahead, and time was running out fast but Huntingdon was making a hard drive down the field and having success. If they scored they would win the game. They were inside the ten yard line; we had to make a stand. The next play I broke through Huntingdon's offensive line and stuck the running back right in his tracks. It was the shot in the arm my team needed. We were so fired up I knew nothing could stop us. We broke through the line again sacking the quarterback. Two more times we had to stop them to win the game, and stop them we did! We had beaten one of our biggest rivals! We were all on cloud nine; it was one of the greatest times of my football career. That night I had the best defensive game of my life. I had several tackles and quarterback sacks that evening. Their line couldn't do anything to stop me, I was a machine. We were so pumped after that game we wanted the next season to arrive so we could be a part of the high school team. Little did I know in the middle of the euphoria that was to be the end of my football career.

Because of my illness I never had the opportunity to play a single down for my high school team. My heart was broken; I ate, drank, and breathed football. All the years I put my heart and soul on the line in practice and during games to reach my goal of playing high school football had all came crashing down.

In 2006, at the start of my freshman year in high school, I became a High School War Eagle. I was finally a member of the high school football team. This was the only year my brother and I were on the same football team. I had so been looking forward to us playing together that year, it was another great disappointment but I dealt with it. I considered myself on the "injured reserve list" and fully intended to return to playing when my treatments were finished. Though I remained unable to play, my coaches and teammates fully included me as part of the team. When it came time for us to get our game jerseys I was hoping to get 67, the number I wore in junior high, but my teammate Jake Goad was already 67. I was disappointed but I would get over it. Jake ended up doing a very unselfish thing and giving up his number 67 jersey. He gave it to my brother Daniel, who also unselfishly gave up his number 64 jersey in order to wear the number 67 in my honor. Daniel told me he wanted to wear my number and play for me that year. I was so humbled. It was Daniel's senior year, his year to be in the spotlight and shine, but he unselfishly gave that up to put me in the spotlight. For these unselfish gestures I will forever be grateful. Thank you Daniel and Jake.

The first time I officially walked on the field as a WCHS War Eagle was at our football jamboree in Huntingdon. Coach Rich and my fellow teammates honored me by asking me to take the field for the coin toss as a co-captain with the senior co-captains. They also honored me by having me run out on the field first at the start of the 2006 homecoming game carrying the WCHS flag.

Throughout my four years of high school I tried my very best to attend every game and stand on the sideline to support my team. The times I was in the hospital on game day I would wear my jersey and at game time I would listen to the game over my aunt's cell phone or call people who were there and get frequent updates.

My school, teammates and coaches went above and beyond to make me feel like a part of them. They dedicated games to me, gave me special honors, and in my darkest hour painted my number on the field and wore decals of my number on their helmets during my senior season. They will never know how much this helped me get through the football seasons; seasons I could not get out on the field and play when that is all I ever wanted to do.

My greatest honor and most humbling moment came near the conclusion of my senior year of high school. After much work on the part of the school administration, football coaches, and my teammates, I was called to school for a presentation to retire my football jersey, number 67. I was extremely humbled and emotionally moved by the things people had to say about me. They will never know how much that moment meant to me. Every time I pass by the West Carroll Football Field, I look over at the press box and from highway 77 I see my jersey hanging there. And each time, I am able to relive those memories.

As I look back, I remember being devastated with the inability to take the field on Friday nights. But, from where I sit now I can't imagine my high school football years being any more memorable than they turned out to be.

On September 1, 2006 I was presented with a Polaris Ranger as my one true wish from the Mid-South Make-A-Wish Foundation and the McKenzie Chapter of the Fellowship of Christian Athletes

On April 19, 2010, West Carroll Special School District and the West Carroll football program honored me by retiring my football jersey, number 67. My jersey now hangs on the back of the press box at War Eagle stadium for all to see. It is the only football jersey to ever be retired in West Carroll History. It was one of the greatest honors in my life. Pictured are Josh Fronabarger; head football coach, Dad, Daniel, Mom, and Lex Suite; West Carroll High School Principal.

#67 Jay Rogers Football Jersey Retired

By Jimmy Gilliam
Sports writer

A special assembly was called by the West Carroll Jr./Sr. High School Principal Lex Suite and the West Carroll Football Program on April 19 as they honored Jay Rogers by retiring his jersey. Rogers is a senior at West Carroll and has battled cancer since the eighth grade.

Following an introduction of Jay to the student body, Suite said "I'd like to thank Elliott Signs and Designs of McLemoresville for the jersey replica that will be displayed in Jay's honor. I'd also like to thank Bobby McAlexander and the Touchdown Club, members past and present, for all of the things they've done to help us with this special day and all the support they give to our program. I'd like to thank the West Carroll Director of Schools Eric Williams for being supportive of the West Carroll football program and this special occasion. I especially want to thank the members of the "Jay's Warriors" group for all they have done for the Rogers family and for West Carroll."

Suite followed by addressing Jay, "The coaching staff and I thought that we could get you up here and surprise you, but as some of the seniors keep telling me there's not that many school days remaining before graduation. Jay, your number "67" is going to be retired. The replica of your jersey will be placed on the back of the press box at the football field so everyone in the parking lot and all of those traveling down Highway 70A will see your name and number which is held in honor as a West Carroll War Eagle for all of time."

Suite continued, "For selection into the Pro Football Hall of Fame, you need 80% of the vote. For the Major League Baseball Hall of Fame, you need 75% of all voters. There are a lot of great athletes at the University of Tennessee and other organizations in the high school, college, and professional ranks that deserve to have their jerseys retired. Usually you will have someone to object for some reason, but what's been so interesting about this particular process is that 100% of the people that I've spoken with about this matter were in total agreement that we need to retire Jay Rogers' jersey and that is a testament to the type of person that Jay is."

"I'm not going to talk a great deal about number 67 the football player," said Suite, "but Jay has played football at West Carroll since the old flag football league some time ago and my son, Carson, also moved through the same ranks around the same time, so I know that some of the emotion that I feel for Jay and his family is personal."

"Jay was one of the people that a young Coach Fronabarger said that he could count on from day one as his starting center and defensive tackle. If any of you have ever played for Coach Fronabarger before, that is very high praise indeed," said Suite.

Suite concluded, "Jay, I believe that I watched all of your junior high football games and it's been difficult for myself and I know that it's been difficult for a lot of you here today to go to West Carroll football games for the past four years without Jay being on the field. How do you handle that? Excelling at a game that you've loved since you were a small child and then not being able to hit the field at all. I haven't had the answer to that, but after watching Jay the past four years I can tell you how to do that and that is to do it the Jay Rogers way.

That's the person that I want to talk about today, Jay Rogers the person. Jay has never complained to me about any of the obstacles that he's faced in life. He's a person that's continued to attend our football games to cheer on his friends and classmates. The only real favor that he or his family has ever asked from me is if they could park close to the football stadium on Friday nights. That is why we are here today to retire the first football number to ever be retired at West Carroll."

Following Suite's opening comments the football coaching staff presented Rogers with the jersey replica that will be installed on the back of the press box for all to see as the student assembly gave Jay a standing ovation.

Jay's father, Tim Rogers, spoke upon Jay's behalf saying, "On behalf of Jay, he thanks each of you very much for this tremendous honor. When we first found out that Jay had cancer, it was the end of the junior high season during his eighth grade year. Jay went through chemo, surgery, and radiation but one of the first things that he asked the doctor was can I play football."

"Because of the complexity of his cancer's location," said Tim Rogers, "the doctor had to remove a couple of Jay's ribs during surgery and the doctor said that it would dangerous for him to play. Jay persisted that we could get a special pad made to protect his side. The following season the cancer came back again. Jay fought through the cancer again the second time and he again asked the doctor if he could play football. The doctor would not recommend such activity for Jay.

It seems like every time that Jay got close to building back up, that awful word (cancer) kept coming back to him. When he was forced to have his brain surgery, I think Jay realized that he would not play football again. But, he never gave up on his teammates."

Tim Rogers gave the assembly an example of such devotion to the West Carroll football program, "Jay was lying at Le Bonheur Children's Medical Center at Memphis after his surgery and my sister (Jana) and several of you here today would call and let Jay listen to the football game on the cell phone. During that game Derek Box was injured and it was all we could do to keep Jay restrained in his hospital bed. He was having a fit because he wanted to be at the game."

Tim Rogers continued, "Jay's blood count was low one rainy Friday night and I had to plead with him to stay home because I was afraid that he'd get sick. But, he wanted to be here and he wanted to play."

"We appreciate all of you so much," Tim Rogers concluded, "this has been a journey that we hope and pray that nobody else has to go through. There have been good moments in this journey as well. Good moments with our family because we've gotten closer. Good moments because we realize what is most important in our lives now. Again, we say thank you and continue to ask God to be with Jay because he has a road ahead of him. A journey that he continues to take and we ask that each of you support and pray for him."

Jay Rogers becomes the very first person to have their number retired in West Carroll football history.

http://westcarroll.tn.wcj.schoolinsites.com

4 Jay's Journey With Hunting

My first spark of interest in the sport of hunting came while listening to my family and friends tell stories about their own hunting adventures. I listened to my Granddaddy Glen, (Boat) tell stories about squirrel hunting. He also told of fishing trips that he, my dad, and, my papaw would take at a place on the Tennessee River called Eagle Creek. My dad and papaw also did a little deer hunting now and then on the family farm. So, I had been around others who had hunted, but I had never really taken an interest in it myself. Then in the fall of 2002, with friends and family anticipating the beginning of hunting season, I decided it was time I took a shot at it myself. Part of what got me hooked on hunting was curiosity. I wanted to know just what was so special about hunting that some people would prepare months in advance to get to go?

As deer season rolled around that year, my dad took me to the woods for the first time. We woke up early in the morning, (which seemed more like the middle of the night) got dressed, collected our guns, and headed for the woods. We were going to a deer stand we had set up a couple of weeks earlier. It was back behind our house, on the family farm. We walked for what seemed like forever in the dark. In the distance you could hear the coyotes howl—not to mention the things rustling through the brush. I had never been out in the woods at that time of the morning, so it was just a little bit spooky in spite of the fact that we had guns with which to protect ourselves. After our middle of the night/early morning walk, we arrived at the tree stand, crawled up the ladder, and sat quietly still just waiting for the "big one" to come along. But the "big one" never showed up! Above and below us, we watched squirrels playing around but there was no sign of a deer. We held out for a couple more hours but ended up returning home empty handed. Though I didn't have any luck either seeing or killing a deer that trip, I kept finding myself anxious to return to the woods to see if my luck would change.

With deer season ending that year, I decided to seriously pursue bagging a deer in the next season. Over the next several months (before the beginning of the next hunting season) I saved my money and bought myself a deer rifle with a scope. My next step was taking and passing the Tennessee Wildlife Resources Agency (TWRA) hunter safety course. My cousin, Zac, and I took the course at the same time. We both passed the written test but when it came to the shooting test we stunk—neither one of us hit a target! However, I now had the right clothes, a gun, and a safety certificate. All I needed was for deer season to arrive.

It was now the fall of 2004 and again my dad took me to the woods on the family farm. Again, we left the warm house, and in the dark we walked a million steps to the a deer stand. It was bitterly cold sitting up in that tree. There was a slight breeze and squirrels were running around everywhere. But again, no luck.

A few days later we returned to the stand while my cousin Zac and Papaw went to a deer stand across the field. As the sun rose and it became lighter, Dad and I heard a shot across the field. It was close, so we knew it was Zac who had taken a shot. Because of where their stand was we were unable to see them, and so, we did not see what he had shot at. We waited up in the tree for what seemed like forever. Dad and I didn't want to leave the stand too early and take the chance of spooking a wounded deer, so we waited. After a few minutes passed we heard a stirring in the woods. I got excited thinking that this would be my big chance to bag a deer! Anxiously, we waited and watched! The sounds got closer, we thought that maybe Zac missed the deer and it was headed our way, or maybe another deer was wandering our way.

As the sounds came closer we saw that it wasn't a deer. It was Zac and Papaw! Dad and I climbed out of the stand and we stood and talked about the morning's events. Zac had taken a shot at a deer but he was hunting with a shotgun loaded with a slug. If you know anything about shotguns and slugs you know they are not very accurate. And so, as your probably have guessed by now, Zac's shot missed and the deer ran off.

I don't remember hunting much that season and though I didn't have any luck bagging a deer, I loved being in the woods and having the anticipation of seeing one.

Days passed quickly and once again deer season was right around the corner. With that being the case, the barrel of my gun was getting hot with all the target practice I was getting in. If I got a deer in my sights this year I was going to make sure I laid it down. On opening day I hit the woods on the farm once again. And once again, day after day we saw nothing! With the arrival of Thanksgiving, one of my favorite holidays, I had a day of food, football, and hunting on the agenda. It was the plan for a perfect day! With extended family in town for the holiday, my cousin Kimberly's husband, Jason McIntyre, offered to carry me to the woods on Thanksgiving morning. Dad said that would be OK with him. I was pretty excited! Jason had done quite a bit of deer hunting, so I hoped to learn a few things from him that might make my trips to the woods a little more productive. Thanksgiving morning Jason and I arrived at the stand early, got situated and waited for the sun to come up. As the sun rose and it became lighter I could see deer at the edge of the field and knew my luck was about to change. Walking up the far side of the fence row was a big buck. I was getting so excited I was about to burst! We watched and waited, but he would not cross the fence so I could get a good shot. Jason and I were really aggravated, but we stayed up in the stand waiting for a break. Finally the break came and out of the woods, on the right side of the fence row, two hundred yards away came a big doe. I knew that this was it! I raised my rifle, and got her in the crosshairs on my scope. Jason later said I was breathing hard and shaking like crazy. I tried to hold the rifle still and slowly squeezed a shot off! The loud noise came from the gun, the deer jumped into the air, ran about thirty feet and fell! I had done it! I had shot my first deer! We waited up in the stand for a while longer to see if anything else would walk out of the woods but nothing else came. I couldn't wait to get down and get a close look at my success!

Jason and I gathered up the deer and headed back to the house so I could show off my prize! She was a good healthy doe weighing about a hundred pounds. We field dressed her and took her back up to Aunt Millie's house, which was on the far end of the farm. Mom, Dad, Daniel, Granny, Papaw, aunts, uncles and cousins all gathered around to admire my success. Mom made numerous pictures of my deer, then Dad, Jason, and I carried it to the processor.

A couple weeks later a picture of me and my deer ended up in the local newspaper. Across the top of it was the headline, "First Deer." My success was now known county wide. It was at that moment the fever hit—"Buck Fever" that is! I have been hunting ever since.

My next hunting trip would not come until the fall of 2006 during the juvenile hunt. My guide was Benjie Lawrence whom I had come to know from attending church at Trezevant. Benjie carried me hunting on his family's land in Henry County, Tennessee. The deer I got on that trip was special because it was the first buck I had ever killed. For a young deer hunter there are two special moments and those moments will appear in your local newspaper, your first deer and your first buck. For some, these two photos may be combined if you are lucky enough for your first kill to be a buck. The hunt in Henry County was to be the shortest trip to the woods I had ever taken. After being in the woods for thirty minutes, we spotted a doe coming out of the tree line into the field. I was tempted to take a shot, but decided to hold off because I really wanted to get a buck this time out. Minutes after spotting the doe, I spied a decent buck following her. It was a young eight point, probably a year and a half or two years old. I raised my rifle and nervously squeezed off a round—and missed. I thought it was going to run off, but to my surprise he didn't. I raised my rifle, took aim, and let another round fly. The deer jumped and ran off into the woods. Benjie and I climbed down from the stand, walked over to the spot where the deer had been standing, and looked over toward the spot where it had run into the woods. Upon first glance into the woods we saw no evidence of success, but as we looked a little closer we saw it laying behind a fallen tree branch. I had gotten him! After a moment of celebration we loaded the buck onto the back of the four wheeler, tied him down, and headed for the truck. After loading the ATV on the trailer, we headed towards home.

While pulling onto the highway, the four wheeler rolled backwards off the trailer and into the middle of the road. The only thing I could think of was, "Please don't let the deer's rack get broken!" Now chuckle as you picture this. Benjie and I jump out of the truck and start chasing a runaway four wheeler with a deer strapped to the back of it down a four lane highway! Benjie was worried about the four wheeler, and I was worried about the deer's rack! I can only imagine what the people passing by watching this were saying. It had to be something like, "Look at those two dummies!" After getting back in the truck we couldn't help but have a few laughs ourselves. It was a true redneck moment.

My coveted second newspaper headline and photo appeared the following week thanks to Benjie's wife, Nichole. As you guessed, this time it read "First Buck." I will always remember this hunting trip as the deer who almost got away...twice! Though I went to the woods many times, that was the only deer I killed that season.

The 2007 season was a little more productive. I killed two does on Melvin and Mildred Pittman's land just outside Trenton, Tennessee, not far from our house.

It was during the summer, several months after deer season ended, that Mom, Dad, and I, on our way back home from Memphis, stopped by the *Gander Mountain*® outdoor store in Jackson. I was looking for a shotgun that was better set up for turkey hunting than what I had at home. While I was shopping, Dad ran into Kevin Hill, or "Catfish" as he is known by most. Dad had come to know him a couple years earlier while they were working together on a job in western Tennessee. As they were talking, I joined in the conversation and told him about my upcoming elk hunt. Before we parted ways, he gave me an invitation to come out to his place in middle Tennessee for a deer hunt in the upcoming season.

My first deer. I killed it on the family farm in Trezevant, TN November 27, 2004.

Benjie Lawrence and me with my first buck. I got it on Benjie's land in Henry County, Tennessee.

In the fall of 2008, with deer season gearing up, I got a call from Catfish inviting me to his home for a weekend of deer hunting. The first morning of hunting, we met one of Catfish's friends, Mike Tucker. They had been watching some of the bucks on Mr. Mike's land and thought the best chance for a trophy buck would be on his place. Early on the last morning of the hunt, we headed out to a pasture behind his house. We came to a hog feeder turned hunting blind. It was mounted fifteen feet in the air and situated on a fence row. The blind faced the woods at the bottom of the mountain where the deer came out into the pasture to feed. That morning as dawn began, the deer started coming down from the mountain. But, all we could see for a while were "slick heads" (does). Knowing that large bucks had regularly been seen in the area, I was told to be patient and keep watching the tree line. Mr. Mike had left the hog feeder and gone behind us to see if he could scare the deer up from the area where they bedded down. He was gone for several minutes and as the morning wore on, finally, out of the woods came a buck. He came out to about the middle of the pasture and began grazing. Through my scope I could see he was a good nine pointer with a tall uniform rack. I was about to burst, I could not believe the rack on this thing! It was time to take my shot! Catfish told me to look at the body and not at the rack on his head and squeeze one off. I thought, "Are you kidding me? Look at that rack!" Never in my life had I ever seen antlers like that on a deer, and I had this bad boy in my crosshairs. I took aim, squeezed the trigger and Bam! He fell dead in his tracks! I literally could have burst with excitement! I had just laid down my first trophy buck. I couldn't wait to get over to size him up! Shortly after he hit the ground, we climbed down from the hog feeder and headed toward him. As we looked across the field, we saw a herd of about fifty deer. We knew Mr. Mike was over that way and that he must have spooked them. As they ran across the field toward the mountain I raised my rifle and shot at them, I still had two does I was allowed to take that day. I aimed, let a round go and one went down. It was a small doe but I was proud I got it. She would help fill up the freezer. I knew it would be good eating.

We called Mom and Dad, and they came and met us at the Tucker's house. When they arrived, we took them with us to the field to gather the deer and make pictures. We started with the buck, gathered him up and put him in the back of Mr. Mike's S-10 pickup. After Mom made a bunch of pictures we headed across several acres of pasture to where the doe had fallen. When we arrived I got a great surprise. There were two deer down just a few feet from one another. I had killed two deer with one bullet! Man, what a morning! One was the doe I had aimed for and the other was a button buck, who unfortunately for him, was in the line of fire.

Ok, now back to the big buck. He had the biggest rack I had ever seen. It was a good, uniform typical nine point with tall brow tines and scored 125. He weighed 150 pounds field dressed. Of course after every good kill you have bragging rounds to make! Catfish and his neighboring landowners are well known in their part of the country for working together to properly manage the deer herds. Because of their cooperation they grow some big, healthy trophy deer. So naturally when a deer is killed on their lands, people are always curious to see what has been taken. On our way to the check-in station we stopped by several neighbor's houses to show off the kill before ending up at Ashley's Quick Stop, a local hangout and check station. It is a popular place for hunters to gather and show off their successful hunt. I had two things to brag about, the big buck and a two for one shot. Funny, no one believed my story of trying to save on expensive ammunition!

The next season I returned to Catfish's mountain and took two does but could never get another shot off at a good buck. I did promise them I would be back next year!

The 2009 deer season was met with even greater success. That year the big bucks wouldn't be as lucky. I aimed for success. I once again returned to Catfish's house for another long weekend in the woods. This year my success didn't come on Catfish's mountain, but an hour west of Belvidere, outside the little town of Fayetteville, Tennessee. We headed to Fayetteville for an afternoon hunt. As we sat in the blind the afternoon wore on and the sun was starting to go down behind the trees. It was then that we saw a big buck come wandering out of the woods. He was coming from the direction of the setting sun making it hard to get a really good look at the size of his rack, but I could see he was a big bodied deer. I decided in an instant that I was going to try to take him down. I raised my rifle, got him in the crosshairs and tried to calm down enough to take a shot. I was shaking so hard with excitement that those crosshairs were going up and down, up and down. I took a deep breath, held it, steadied myself, and squeezed the trigger! With the sound of the round going off I lowered my gun and watched the big buck fall straight in his tracks. Catfish and I got down from the blind and walked towards where the deer lay. When I got a good look at him, I saw he was huge. In the years I had hunted I had never seen such a big deer. He had big thick antler beams and was a twelve point, mature deer. Catfish figured by looking at him he was probably a four and a half or five year deer—old for a deer. He was without a doubt the boss in his neck of the woods! He scored just under 150 and weighed in at 225 pounds.

In 2010, I again returned to the woods of Belvidere with Catfish. I missed the big buck but took down four does and filled the freezer with meat. Over the years I have thoroughly enjoyed spending time with Catfish. I have stood in amazement of his "luck." It seems like he always finds the biggest buck, flock of turkey, or the largest fish in the lake. But after listening to, and watching him, for so long, it is not "luck" as one would think. He has a dedicated himself to learning about these animals, their needs, and their habits. His "luck" didn't just happen, but it came with a lot of hard work. I have learned so much about "the hunt" from him.

October 27, 2007 hunt on the Pittman Farm in Gibson County, Tennessee.

Kevin "Catfish" Hill, Mike Tucker, and me with a nine pointer on the Tucker Farm in Huntland, Tennessee.

Kevin "Catfish" Hill, Trey Childs, and me with a **12** pointer killed on the Childs' Farm in Fayetteville, Tennessee.

Kevin "Catfish" Hill and me, Spring **2009** turkey hunt, Belvidere, Tennessee.

It is at this point in the chapter I feel I need to tell you a little information I chose to leave out until I could talk about my elk hunt and the circumstances that allowed me to go on it. All of my hunting trips, except for the first doe I killed on our farm, were not just a challenge because I was trying to outsmart the animal but because I was being treated for bone cancer. While on these hunts I fought nausea, pain, weakness, and fatigue. Most times I could not walk long distances, climb up a tree stand, or hold up my gun to take a shot without difficulty. My guides and hunting partners were all really great about "going the extra mile" to accommodate my physical limitations. But fighting through it was all worthwhile because I loved the hunt. Most times, if I spent a weekend hunting I was wiped out for the following week. Enough of that! I'll go into greater detail of my struggles with my health in a later chapter. But for now, let's go back to hunting.

The crown jewel of all my hunting experiences was my Wyoming elk hunt. I say that not because the others were any less a good time, but because the scope of this hunt was on such a larger scale and so different from what I would have ever been able to do if I had not been diagnosed with cancer. Not many Tennessee boys I know have been fortunate enough to say they have been elk hunting out west.

It was the fall of 2006, between the Thanksgiving and Christmas holidays, while in the Transplant unit at St. Jude Children's Research Hospital that I was visited by Stephen Dorris. He had heard of me by way of Mrs. Sharon Wright, who is a member of the church I attended and who also worked for a man who is

involved with Mr. Dorris' *Hunting Hearts Foundation.*
On a somewhat local level, the *Hunting Hearts*
Foundation provides hunting experiences for kids who
are seriously handicapped or who have a life
threatening illness. Mr. Dorris told me he had heard all
about me and my love of hunting from Mrs. Sharon and
wanted to come explain to me what his foundation
does. Before our visit ended, he gave me a pamphlet
from another wish granting foundation based out of
Mississippi State University's main campus. It is known
as the *Catch-A-Dream Foundation.* He explained to me
that he was also involved with this foundation and
many of his *Hunting Hearts* wish recipients were also
granted trips through the *Catch-A-Dream Foundation.*
He told me how to contact them, gave me one of their
applications, I filled it out and sent it in.

The *Catch-A-Dream* application asked one
question. They wanted to know what my one true
hunting or fishing dream trip was. Boy, this took some
thought. I had so many places to which I wanted to go
and so many different animals I wanted to hunt. It
would be a hard task to narrow it down to one. I knew
that whatever I went after, it had to be a trip that was
somewhere I had never been and an animal that was a
lot bigger or more dangerous than what I could hunt in
west Tennessee. After "hem-hawing" around I finally
made the big decision. I wanted to hunt grizzly bear in
Alaska! I thought, "Now that would be the ultimate
hunting trip. You can't get any farther out of west
Tennessee than Alaska, or any more dangerous than
grizzly bears."

About a week after I submitted my application I received a call from the *Catch-A-Dream Foundation*. They expressed some concerns over such a hunt. Their first concern was that they had never had a fourteen year old ask to hunt an animal this dangerous. Their second concern was about how my family would be able to be involved in such a hunt. It was important to me that Mom, Dad, and Daniel were along to experience this with me. After some discussion on the matter, the wish coordinator explained that I really needed to make a choice as to whether I would rather hunt a grizzly or experience a hunt with my family. They said they would try and get some more information from an outfitter to see if my request was even doable. They also said they would let me think over some other hunt options and then contact me again in a few days. I knew before I hung up the phone that it was more important to me to experience a hunt with my family then hunt a bear. I later discovered there were many other factors that would not allow me to hunt bear, such as time of season and the difficulty involved in hunting such an animal.

I had spent much time in thought about what would be my one true hunting wish. If I couldn't have a nice bear rug, I wanted a huge rack of antlers to go on the wall. I wanted to hunt elk! When the *Catch-A-Dream* coordinator called me back, I told him my wish and he said that would make a great family adventure. Dates were set, tickets were bought, and I geared up for the hunt.

I was going to Gillette, Wyoming to hunt elk. I was so excited! I was going somewhere I had only dreamed of going and hunting an animal that was one of the biggest animals in North America. In November, 2007 we left Trenton early in the morning and headed to Memphis International Airport. We boarded the "big bird" and headed out west! Our flight was in two legs. We landed in Denver after about a two and a half hour flight. What a place! In my life I had never seen such an airport and so many people all rushing here and there and walking so fast. Daniel and I had the best time on the moving sidewalk! If you walked fast on it you were really moving on! Sorry, I guess I don't have to tell you I'm from the country, huh? Anyway the folks in the airport told us we would have to go down to the bottom level to catch a train that would take us to the terminal to board the flight to Gillette.

I just knew we would never make it! I couldn't believe we were in a place so big that you had to ride a train to get to other parts of it! Well, Mom figured it all out, and we found where to board the flight to Wyoming with plenty of time to spare.

It was at the gate to our flight that we were to meet Cliff Covington, our host from *Catch-A-Dream*. He was there to take care of everything—from the hotel, to the meals and sightseeing and even to helping on the hunt. Dad had talked to him on the phone a few times and knew where and when we would meet, but we had no idea what he looked like—not the first clue. I got tickled because we sat lined up in the terminal checking everyone out as they came by the airline desk, trying our best to decide if they were Cliff. We acted like cops hunting a fugitive. Finally Dad, being a little nervous we would miss Cliff and our flight, began walking up and down the terminal asking men who looked like they were waiting for someone if they were Cliff. It was so funny to watch him. I guess Cliff could pick us out with no problem since he spotted us right away. Go figure! What a bunch of hicks!

We boarded our flight to Gillette, arriving that afternoon with no problems. At the Gillette airport we met up with our hunting guide, Mr. Steve Beilgard. He took us to get checked into our hotel and helped us get our luggage to our rooms. Mr. Steve was really friendly and excited about our arrival and upcoming hunt. He talked with a strange accent—it wasn't southern. I don't know if you would call it a yankee accent or what? I guess he thought I talked strange too.

We quickly hit it off and started talking hunting. Later in the conversation he left and came back with a funny looking brass horn and told me if I was going to hunt elk I needed to practice my elk call. He handed me the horn and told me to blow hard. I knew it didn't look like anything you would call a deer with but he was the expert, I had to trust him. I blew as hard as I could and ended up with a face full of baby powder! I should have known better! I knew then he was going to be a trickster! I thought of revenge right away. What could I do to get him back? We started talking about the upcoming hunt so I put that thought on the back burner, hunting first, then revenge!

After we got our rooms and luggage squared away, and I cleaned the baby powder off my face, we headed to the firing range for a little target practice. I was going to use Mr. Steve's gun the next morning on the hunt and I wanted to be familiar with it. There was no way I was going to miss a good one if I had him in my sights. The rifle felt good and I hit within the bullseye several times. I was now ready to face down an elk.

Bright and early the following morning, Mr. Steve, his son-in-law, Jeff, and grandson, Kaeden showed up at the hotel to pick us up. Though I had trouble falling asleep the night before, I had no trouble waking up that morning. Shortly after the alarm clock went off, my family and I were up, dressed, and ready to go hunting in the Wyoming backcountry.

I soon discovered that in Wyoming they don't hunt like we do in Tennessee—especially west Tennessee. Instead of sneaking into the woods and going to a tree stand or blind, they stalk the animals. I didn't know what in the world to expect as to the method of hunting. I did know that my family would be able to go on the hunt and that hunting the way I was used to would be difficult with a crowd of people. We loaded up in four wheel drive vehicles and off we went.

The region I was assigned to hunt was on a privately owned cattle ranch outside the town of Gillette. Mr. Steve knew the owner and had knowledge of the elk herds that lived in the area. He had done his homework before we had gotten there. The owner, Mr. Tracey, told us where to find the gates in the fences so we could make our way through the pastures to the area where the elk roamed. It was so strange to hear someone talk about their land and its size in relation to miles! I have never known anyone who could talk about traveling across their land in that large a distance. When we left the canyon where Mr. Tracey's house was located and drove up on the hill to enter the pasture I could not believe how far we could see. All this land was where I was going to hunt! I was also surprised that the landscape was able to support grazing animals of any kind, it was so rocky and dry. They didn't have grass as I knew it but instead it was sage brush and other strange looking grasses. There weren't many trees either, just a few clumps of pines and cottonwoods here and there but no woods and forests like I was accustomed to. You could look across the way and see for miles.

Anyway, we continued cross country toward the last whereabouts of the elk herd. We drove up and down hills, over mountains and through gullies, places I would have never dreamed of driving a vehicle. We would drive a little ways then stop and search for the elk with a spotting scope. I don't really know how far you could see with the scope but it was a really long way, further than I would have ever dreamed of seeing.

Not long after we arrived in the back country, as the sun was beginning to rise, we spotted three elk walking across a ridge. It was like a scene out of a movie. It was all just so beautiful—the prettiest picture I had ever seen. And too, I was amazed at how big the elk looked in the distance. Mr. Steve pulled out the spotting scope to see the size of the animals. He said it was a good size animal so we jumped back into the truck and went to head them off.

After a few minutes we were able to drive around and get in position in the direction the elk were headed. We got out of the trucks and I got ready to take a shot. We laid down behind the ridge the elk were walking below and waited for them as they came closer. They were moving pretty fast and the closer they got the more nervous I became. When they came around the ridge and got closer the lay of the land kept me from getting a good shot. We hurriedly got back in the truck to come around where we thought they would come out from behind the ridge, but they ended up getting away from us, we never saw them again.

We continued traveling over the land, glassing with the scope for the remainder of the morning without any luck. We took a break and drove into a nearby town for lunch and returned to the ranch that afternoon. While heading back out into the middle of nowhere I could not believe how many wild animals we saw—coyote, eagles, and many herds of mule deer and pronghorn antelope. It was a hunters dream. We also scared up some jack rabbits. They were huge. I have never, ever seen a rabbit that size. They were as big as beagle dogs. It was unreal! Every now and then we would come across a herd of Mr. Tracey's cattle.

We continued on through the afternoon and finally came across a herd of about 20 elk. Mr. Steve spotted them off in the distance, bedded down on the top of a mountain. Both trucks stopped and we got out and watched them for a few minutes. We were also on the top of a mountain and even though it was so far off in the distance they had also noticed us. And so, as we watched them they in turn watched us back.

After much discussion on our strategy of attack, a decision was made and we began stalking the herd. It took us quite a long time to travel cross country to get where we needed to be. But by the time we got there, they were already on the move and heading right in our direction!

It was getting close to sundown. I was nervous and my adrenaline was pumping. In other words, I was "tore up"! I was afraid we would lose light before I could get a shot at one. They had come down off the mountain on our right side and crossed the gulley we were driving in directly in front of us. They quickly started up the mountain to the left of us trying to get away. The bull, or male elk, got halfway up the mountain trailing behind several cow, or female elk. He stopped to look back at a few cow elk that were behind him and waited for them to catch up and pass him. When he did this I took aim and busted him! I squeezed off a few more shots until he went down. I had done it!

After a short celebration and enthusiastic hug from Kaeden, we all headed to where the elk lay. It was further than it looked, about 250 yards away. It was hard to walk that far because of the elevation. The air was thin and I had just had lung surgery three weeks prior to our trip. But no way was I going let that stop me! The closer we got to the elk the more I couldn't believe the size of it. It was huge. He had a great looking rack, a 6x7. In Tennessee we would have called him a 13 pointer, scoring around 300. It was the biggest rack I had ever laid my eyes on! Mr. Steve said that it was in the top twenty percent harvested in that area that season. Everyone celebrated with me. We made a ton of pictures with Mr. Steve, my guide, Mr. Jeff, Kaeden, Cliff from *Catch-A-Dream*, and my family. I was grinning like a possum!

It was now time to get down to business. The elk had to be field dressed and gotten down off the mountain before the sunset and the coyotes smelled blood and became curious. This was going to be a chore. The elk weighed around 900 pounds and the loose rocky ground on the mountain made it hard to walk, let alone carry down 900 extra pounds. Mr. Steve made quick work of gutting him and he, Mr. Cliff, Jeff, Dad, and Daniel began to drag him down the hill. They quickly found out he was too heavy to get down in one piece. Dad was holding the elk by the horns and backing down when it kind of got away from them and gouged him in the stomach. Mr. Steve then took out his knife, felt down the backbone, found the spot he wanted and went to cutting. In no time flat he had it cut in two. The elk was then safely gotten down the mountain and loaded into the truck. We drove cross country back to the house of the ranch owner, Mr. Tracey, to show off my trophy and thank him for allowing me to hunt on his land. We took the kill to the processor/taxidermist and discussed the particulars of how I wanted the head mounted.

Our trip to Wyoming was scheduled to last seven days. Since I killed my elk on the first hunting day we had five days for sightseeing. Cliff, our host took us to many places that I had only dreamed of seeing. We drove to Montana to see where Custer's last stand took place at the battleground of Little Big Horn. In South Dakota, We visited Mount Rushmore National Monument, Sturgis, home of the world famous biker rally, and Deadwood, the home of Wild Bill Hickock.

We also toured the Big Thunder coal mine outside Gillette, Wyoming. The equipment used in the mine was on an unbelievably huge scale. Dump trucks were so big you could walk under them. We saw one piece of equipment called a drag line which is used to dig huge amounts of dirt and coal out of the ground. This particular drag line, that we were able to go into, happened to be the largest one ever made and was featured on the Discovery Channel's show, *Modern Marvels*. We got to walk through it and see how it worked. They showed us the cockpit and let me sit in the operators seat, boy I could have tore up jack with that thing! After an exciting week in Wyoming, we boarded a plane and returned home with two large coolers of meat in tow. What a wonderful experience we had. It was unforgettable!

Catch-a-Dream wish trip to Gillette, Wyoming November 2007. 6x7, 900 lb. bull elk. Pictured are Steve Beilgard, my hunting guide; Cliff Covington, *Catch-A-Dream* sponsor and guide and me.

In October 2008, I headed out to Wisconsin to hunt black bear. Instead of flying we decided to drive. Again my family and I were able to see country we had never seen before. We drove through Illinois which was flat and full of cornfields as far as the eye could see. We stopped in Springfield to visit the grave of Abraham Lincoln and stretch our legs before we continued on to Wisconsin. We were headed to Hayward which was in northern Wisconsin, 90 miles south of the southern shore of Lake Superior. Our trip was arranged by *United Special Sportsman's Alliance*, based in Wisconsin.

Our host and taxidermist, Mr. Jeremy Hage and hunting guides, Mr. Dave, Mrs. Annette, Mr. Mooney, and their Redbone Coonhounds met us the day after our arrival and took us to the woods several miles outside Hayward. I thought it was so funny that you hunt bear with coon dogs. The dogs were taken by leash to the woods to pick up the bear's scent, When they caught it they were released and off they went into the distance running and sounding off! The hunt was on! They were hot on the trail. Each dog wore a collar with a tracking device so the owners could keep up with where they were. After quite a lengthy run we heard them in the distance and headed in their direction. The forest floor was unlike anything I had ever walked over, much different from the woods of Tennessee. The forest was very dense with a lot of smaller trees and bushes and though we were not in bottom lands, the forest floor was soft and spongy making it more difficult to walk. Finally we made it to where the bear was. I used the guide's gun—a 500 caliber deer rifle. I guess they wanted to make sure I killed the bear and not just make him mad! You could have killed a bull elephant with that thing! As you guessed, my luck was good. I harvested my first black bear.

Another memorable hunt on which I was privileged to go was in the late fall of 2009. I went hunting for Russian Boar in Fayetteville, Tennessee. This animal was also hunted with dogs, Mountain Cur, and had a reputation for being an ornery critter too. Like the elk hunt, my family was able to go with me to the woods. We met our guide, Mr. Stacey Smith, and others with his dogs and took to the woods. The dogs caught the scent of the boar and shortly tracked him down along with several sows and their young. We followed the dogs all through woods, some fields, and even through a pond, and finally came upon where they had the boar held up hiding in a thicket of brush. The dogs were finally able to run the hogs out of the thicket where they then ran into a pond and swam to the other side.

I didn't shoot while the boar was in the pond, If I had killed him while in the water he would have sunk to the bottom. When the boar swam out of the pond he ran right into another thicket. He held up there for a pretty good while. The boar stayed hidden for a long time so the three hunting guides went into the thicket to encourage him to come out. Mr. Stacey crawled on top of the brush pile, held onto a tree branch above him, and began to jump and shake the pile.

Next thing I knew the boar was coming after us! Dad shoved me behind him, and the boar ran right past us. It didn't miss us by much, only a foot or so. All I could think was "Thank you Dad!" The things a dad will do to keep his "younguns" safe! Daniel, Catfish, Mr. Stacey, and the other guides ran away from him and a couple of them even climbed trees to get out of its reach!

Mom had been in a *Polaris Ranger*® beside the brush pile when the boar came running out. She saw it was headed right for her and climbed up on the seat of the *Ranger.* She refused to get out of the vehicle the remainder of the hunt.

The boar ran away with the dogs trailing behind it. We walked what seemed like a couple miles, again, catching up with the dogs and hogs. This time we hung back in the cover of the woods. It was at this point I was able to get off a shot. I was hunting with Catfish's crossbow and I knew if I didn't hit him in the right spot he would really be mad. I took my time, aimed, and squeezed the trigger. I hit the boar in the right spot, he ran a few feet and went down. He was a good mature boar, weighing about 250 pounds. After all the picture making and thanking all those involved I was worn slap out! Since the hunt, I have been asked what I would have done if I had missed a good shot on the boar. My response is "I was not going to miss!"

I know some have reservations when it comes to hunting animals. All the animals I have harvested have been not only for the trophies to put on the wall, but to also put food in my family's freezer. I believe in being a responsible hunter and good steward of the bounties God has given us to enjoy. At no time would I ever hunt an animal I did not have the intention of using for food. I have been very fortunate to have been given opportunities to go to so many different places to hunt many different species of animals. I realize that many will never get the opportunity to do what I have been given the chance to do. Many people have been involved and sacrificed to make these experiences possible for me to enjoy. I am so thankful to you all. My family and I will cherish those memories forever.

Black Bear, Hayward, Wisconsin, October 2008. This hunt was made possible through the efforts of the United Special Sportsman's Alliance of Wisconsin.

Kevin "Catfish" Hill and me with a 250 pound Russian Boar killed in Fayetteville, Tennessee on October 27, 2008. This hunt was made possible by Stacey Smith of Tennessee Extreme Outdoor Adventures.

5 Jay's Journey With Cancer

Cancer.

How can one word be so powerful that it always, and without question, turns your head and makes you sit up and take notice when it is mentioned? Once that word and your name are spoken in the same sentence in a doctor's office, your life immediately, at that very moment, changes forever. In an instant, it takes away your life as you know it, and as you imagined it would be in the future. You no longer will wake up to a morning that has the same simple monotonous routine as it did the day before. You long to live those long days you thought were so ordinary and filled with so many problems again. As the saying goes, "You hit a brick wall."

In November of 2005, at the age of thirteen, my life was forever changed. As I look back on my journey with cancer, I have come to realize that not all of those changes were bad. Many positive things have come as a result of my illness and made me the young man I am today.

It was a routine morning, like any other morning, that most of us have. At thirteen, I was awakened bright and early—at 6:00 a.m. on the dot. It was a school day. Mom always woke us up a little early because we had a few chores to take care of before we left for school at 7:10. Daniel's and my beds had to be made, the goats seen after, and Buck, our dog, had to be let out before we left the house for the day. The school day went much the same as always. After school, when we arrived home in the afternoon, we had to finish our chores which consisted of feeding our outside dogs, of which we had two: Rex our chocolate lab and Babe our border collie. We had to again feed and water the goats, and walk the inside dog. After that, we had to finish our homework, go to ball practice, or maybe just have some free time to play. Mom would cook supper and we would all eat together around the table. Then, we might spend the rest of the night outside or if it was wintertime, we might watch a little television. On Wednesdays, the same routine applied but we always made time to attend Bible study at 7:00 p.m. I never missed Bible study or worship to practice or play a ball game—it was not allowed in my house— God always came first. Most evenings, Mom was busy fixing supper, while at the same time doing laundry or other household chores. Dad would come home after work, go through the mail, do things that needed taking care of around the house, and see what Daniel and I were up to. Most days of my life went much the same.

I had been having trouble with a sore shoulder on and off for a couple of weeks. I had been to the doctor to have it checked out. He thought it was a football injury; a separated shoulder. It would bother me for a couple days following my weekly football game but feel better with a little *Tylenol*® and rest. After another hard hitting game, the same discomfort would return and subside a day or two later.

It was during the weeks this pain was coming and going that I also came down with a typical head cold. After a few days of feeling really bad with chest congestion caused by the cold, I woke up one night with a pain in my lower right side. It hurt really bad when I breathed, and made me feel like I was short of breath. Feeling short of breath scared me, but Mom calmed me down and gave me some *Tylenol*® for the pain. It helped, so we waited till morning to see the doctor. That morning, Mom said after she arrived at work she would call and get me a doctor's appointment and then pick me up from school later. I felt better so there was no need to stay home. Daniel and I had school, and Mom was needed at work. So, off we went to school and work the same as any other normal day.

Later that morning, Mom left West Carroll Primary School where she works, and told them she would be back when we were finished at the doctor's office. She checked me out at the junior high school and told the receptionist, Ms. Lissie Robinson, that I would be back after the appointment. I didn't really feel bad enough to not go back after seeing the doctor, but I had hoped Mom would not make me. Knowing Mom, I knew my luck on that would probably not be too good! Mom said she recalls telling me my pain was probably in some way related to the "crud" I had come down with several days earlier. The doctor would probably give me some meds and maybe even a shot and I could return to school. Yes, even at thirteen I hated the thought of getting a shot!

I had never had much experience with doctor "stuff." I had always been a pretty healthy kid, just the normal, run of the mill sicknesses. I had, however, had one previous experience with needles. I was a pretty good size kid when Dad had to hold me down for a shot. Dad said even then, trying to hold me down to get that shot was like wrestling a bear. He said, when the doctor was finished giving it, both of us were wringing wet with sweat from the struggle. Dad said that episode got a little embarrassing for Mom and him. They both said I put on quite a production.

Back to that day Mom and I were headed to the doctor. Though I don't remember it, Mom recalled us discussing what we would do that afternoon when we got home from school. We always had some kind of project going on at home.

As doctor visits usually go, we waited, and waited, and waited to be called back to see the doctor. Since my appointment was made on short notice, we were unable to see our regular family doctor, Dr. Merrick. Instead, we saw a Dr. Bryant who had just started working in Dr. Merrick's office. After telling him what had been going on, he thought maybe the cold had settled in my chest. He decided to have a chest X-ray made to rule out pneumonia. I went to the back of the office, had my X-ray picture made, then returned to the exam room to wait for the doctor to read the films. Shortly after I got back to the room, the doctor came through the door and Mom and I both sensed that something was terribly wrong. We looked at each other and then back to him to hear the verdict. Never in my wildest dreams did I ever imagine that what he had to say would be so devastating. He proceeded to tell Mom and me that the X-ray showed a mass in my upper right chest cavity. He said he was going down to the CT scan room to have a scan set up for me.

Mom and I sat there dumbfounded. I really didn't know what to think, but I sensed something was not right from watching Mom's face as she called Dad. At the time, he was working as an inspector for a civil engineering company. His job site was about an hour drive from home, so it took him a while to meet up with us in McKenzie, Tennessee where the clinic was located. We sat in the exam room for about forty-five minutes to an hour waiting for Dad and for the CT scanner to become available.

It was one of the scariest times of my life. Though Mom did good holding it together, I knew she was really scared. I really didn't know what it would be that was in my chest, but I did know that masses and cancer were mentioned as being one and the same. I had heard Mom and Dad mention their grandfathers' passing away after they got cancer. In general, I knew that it was a bad and serious disease, and that many people had died, or were dying from it. I remember being comforted by the thought that kids don't get cancer— just older people. I thought to myself that the doctor would figure it out, give me some medicine, possibly even a shot to fix it, and I would be back doing my regular everyday thing again tomorrow.

It seemed like we sat in that room forever before Dad arrived. Shortly after his arrival, the CT scan machine was ready for me. Mom, Dad, and I walked down the hall to a room with this huge machine. It had a hole in the center and a bed sticking out of that hole. It looked really intimidating—like some kind of torture machine.

They had me lie on the table and told me to be very still so the pictures would come out good. The tech tried to send everyone out of the room besides me, but Mom and Dad wanted one of them to stay with me. Dad stayed and talked me through the process. We returned to the exam room and after several minutes the doctor entered with very upsetting news. In his opinion he believed the large mass might be cancerous, but, he said this was far from his specialty and he was not sure. He had set up an appointment with a pediatric surgeon in Memphis for the following morning. He gave us the appointment times, the X-rays and CT scan films. We all left stunned. I felt that everyone was looking at me as we walked out of the office. Later I was told that Dr. Bryant was so upset with the news he had to give us that he left the office shortly after we did and took the rest of the day off. I remember him being very kind through the whole process. I am very thankful to him for that, and for reacting so quickly to get us to Memphis and eventually to St. Jude Children's Research Hospital.

I don't remember how everyone was told or found out about the news we had been given. But, I know it traveled fast. When we arrived home, some of our family members were there waiting on us along with friends and church members who came by throughout the evening. I remember thinking, "This is just a bad dream and tomorrow things will be back to normal." The morning came, and we headed to Memphis. It was a long, fairly quiet drive. All and all, I still clung to that sliver of hope that I did not have cancer.

Our first appointment was with a surgeon in Memphis. A couple months later, Dr. Eubanks, who worked in that same office, would do surgery to remove my tumor. I don't remember much about the appointment, just that he said we needed to go to St. Jude and he would make the arrangements.

I had never spent much time at a doctor's office, let alone a hospital, and I didn't know anything about St. Jude. I vaguely remember seeing the commercials on television showing kids with no hair walking up and down colorful hallways pushing poles with bags hanging from them. It didn't look like a hospital because the kids were all smiling and seemed to be having fun. One thing I do remember is that when those commercials were on and Mom came into the room she would have to change the channel. She told me she couldn't watch them because they upset her so much, and that she couldn't imagine Daniel or me being sick like that. I never knew they had cancer, just that they were sick. Mom did tell me sometime later that she knew St. Jude was a cancer hospital.

When we arrived at St. Jude, we entered through the main lobby. We were looking for the registration desk. As we passed through the lobby, I couldn't help but stare. I was shocked by all the kids I saw who were bald, walking with crutches, riding in wheelchairs, and pushing IV poles around with several bags of medicines hanging from them. I couldn't help but think that would probably be me looking like that in the near future. It was then I knew this was serious business. The distance from the front door to the registration desk was the longest walk of my life. Again, the brick wall

Once through the lobby, we arrived at the registration desk. It wasn't just one desk, but three. They were set up like checkout lines at a grocery store. Mom, Dad, and I waited in line for a few minutes before it was my turn to check in. Mom told them my name and explained that we had an appointment with Dr. Santana. The lady at the desk typed my name in the computer and the printer spat out a tag that was put on a bracelet which was wrapped around my wrist. She began explaining to me that the bracelet had my name, clinic, doctor's name, and a medical record number on it, 22898. I was the twenty-two thousandth, eight hundred and ninety-eighth patient to enter St. Jude Children's Research Hospital. She explained that every time I would enter the hospital from that moment on people would ask me for that number.

We were met at the registration desk by a nurse whose name was Bridgett. She was very kind to me and my family. She spent the day walking us through the process of becoming a new patient at St. Jude. After finishing up at registration, we went on to see patient services, social workers, and then to D Clinic to meet my doctor, fellow, nurse practitioner, nurse, and NCA (nursing care assistant).

First, I met my doctor, Dr. Lisa McGregor and her fellow, Dr. Jessica Roberson. I remember Dr. McGregor being very kind to me. She talked to me like a friend in words I was able to understand. I knew at that time I could trust her to do her very best to take care of me. She talked to me directly about the situation instead of talking to my parents about me like I wasn't there. She asked me what I wanted to know about this very scary situation in which I found myself, and took quite a bit of time to answer my, and my parents, questions. She and her fellow, Dr. Roberson, told me that over the course of the next few days I would go through many tests and biopsies. We would then return to her for the results of all the tests. And, depending on what the tests revealed, she would talk with us about treatment options. For the next couple of days we spent a lot of time on our knees praying to God. Even at this point my family and I were still hoping it was not cancer.

Looking back, it is funny what you remember when you first meet people. One moment I recall was meeting Dr. Roberson, the fellow, or "feller" as I called her. In the south a "feller" is a man. My "feller" was a woman! I remember being very confused about why they were calling this lady doctor a "feller." I later found out Dr. Roberson was called a "feller" because she was taking part in a program that was called a "fellowship," therefore she was a fellow!

Dr. Roberson and I became great friends. We joked a lot about my hunting adventures, my goats, and living in the country. On one of my visits, she told me she would be gone for a couple weeks, she and her family were making a trip to Italy. I asked her if she would bring me back an "Italy" goat. She told me she would smuggle one back in her suitcase just for me. When I saw her in clinic after her return, she came in with a small gift—a little plastic goat! My "Italy" goat! We had a good laugh over it! I have kept that little goat over the past several years. I keep it at the top of my bulletin board. I look at it nearly every day, and I can't help but smile when I see my "Italy goat." Dr. Roberson finished her "fellership" after my initial year of treatment. She moved to Florida to work at a children's hospital in Orlando. I have heard that she still keeps up with me and signs my website from time to time.

Back to my first days at St. Jude. After meeting my doctors and nurses in D Clinic, Mrs. Bridgett came back to get us and carried us to another place in the hospital called Assessment Triage. It is a place I have come to know very well. Generally, it is the first stop that St. Jude patients make to begin their day at the hospital. Almost every visit I have at St. Jude begins with a visit to Assessment Triage. It is the place where I began what would be the start of countless needle sticks, and on this day, my very first day as a St. Jude patient, this is how it began. The nurses at Assessment Triage had to put in an IV line that I would need for a battery of tests. Over the next few days, I had countless tubes of blood drawn, X-rays, CT, PET and bone scans, MRI's with and without contrast from head to toe, and eye, ear and pulmonary function tests. These were some of the most frightening and exhausting few days I can ever remember having. But, the most frightening day was when my family and I were called into the D Clinic exam room to receive the results of all the tests I had undergone.

The day I received my results began the same as the previous days. My family and I arrived at the hospital early that morning after spending the night in the Memphis Grizzlies House on the St. Jude Campus. We checked in at registration and walked down the hall to the D Clinic waiting room. It was filled with my family and friends who had traveled to Memphis to be with us when I was to receive the news that would forever change every aspect of my life. My name was called on the intercom system to report to D Clinic. We left our family and friends, many huddled in prayer, and Mom, Dad, Daniel, and I walked into the small exam room, sat down, and waited for the news. Shortly after being escorted to the exam room, Drs. McGregor and Roberson came in. I could tell by the look on their faces that whatever the news was, it was not good.

As I look back, I realize I didn't really know much about cancer. I only knew that the reaction on people's faces and their conversation when talking about those who had cancer was not a good one. It usually involved the description of brutal chemotherapy treatments, disfiguring surgeries, and death, but the conversation never involved kids having cancer, and kids dying, only adults, older adults.

Dr. McGregor explained that the growth in my chest was a type of bone cancer called Ewings Sarcoma. My family and I were given all the statistics and what could be done to try to cure my disease. Drs. McGregor and Roberson left us alone for a few minutes to digest the information we had been given. I can remember thinking, "I can't have cancer...I'm only thirteen...I'm not old yet...I'm just a kid...Kids don't have cancer." Again, the brick wall. We cried and cried, and hugged one another. I remember Mom, Dad, and Daniel being very upset. It scared me because Mom and Dad were so scared, and if Mom and Dad were that scared, it had to be bad. I knew I should be scared too. When the Doctors returned, we were given a treatment plan and told what the first step in that plan would be. They wasted no time in getting started on the treatment plan. I still hoped that when I woke up the next morning this would all have been a bad dream and I could step back into my life exactly where I stepped out. This just couldn't be happening to me!

Again, it didn't happen, and when I woke up the next morning, the nightmare continued! I was scheduled to take the first step in the treatment plan Drs. McGregor and Roberson had talked about a few days earlier. I had to have surgery to have a "central line" installed. The thing that was about to be put into me was called a "Hickman Double Lumen Intravenous Catheter." It would be put in a large vein close to my heart. This would be the line through which I would receive chemo fluids and countless other medications. I was shown the device and they explained in detail about it and that most "St. Jude Kids" had some type of intravenous device, whether it was a "Hickman" line or a port. I was also told that after completion of my treatment protocol and clear scans six months after my treatments that the line could be removed. Even before it was put in, I was looking forward to the day it would come out. The thought of this tube sticking out of my chest really bothered me. This was to be the first of many surgeries I would have to endure over the coming years. For nearly two years I would have that tube, which meant I had to have dressing changes every Monday, Wednesday, and Friday, and there could be no swimming and no showers—only baths in the tub. It could not get wet because of risk of infection. An infection meant an immediate admission to the hospital.

My initial treatment consisted of chemotherapy courses that would be given over fifty two weeks, a major surgery to remove the tumor, seven weeks of radiation therapy, and a bone marrow transplant. I recall my first overnight hospital stay at St. Jude. It was the day I would receive my first round of chemo-therapy. Up until this time, all my surgeries and tests were on an outpatient basis. I went in for my visit with the doctor in D Clinic. I was checked out and given the all clear to start chemo. Ms. Monica, my D Clinic CNA escorted me to my room up on the second floor of the hospital. I believe the room number was 2073. I would stay there for the next four days. St. Jude's inpatient rooms are divided into two wings. The leukemia and blood disorder patients are on 2 North and the Solid Tumor patients on 2 South. I was on 2 South. My cancer is a solid tumor. Everyone was very nice and tried very hard to help me cope with my first inpatient stay. It would be the first of many to come. After my nurse asked me a countless number of questions, she hooked me up to fluids. I had to be hydrated properly before she was able to start my chemo. The sooner I got started, the sooner I could get out of there. The medication I was to receive was called Doxorubicin. It was to be pumped into me over a 24 hour period. When they started the pump and the red liquid began to be pumped into my system, it scared me to death. It didn't take too long for me to start feeling nauseated. Maybe some of this feeling was just the thought of this poison being pumped in me. For whatever the cause, nauseated is how I began to feel. To counteract the nausea I was given several medications all of which made me very drowsy. The medications knocked me out and I slept most of the night. The morning came, and I began to feel some discomfort in my shoulder. I did not know it at the time, but when cancer cells die they swell. The tumor was already so large it was compressing one third of my lung. So, needless to say, there was not much room in my chest for it to expand. I began to hurt and with each passing hour I hurt even more. The pain became so excruciating I cried and begged for some relief. The doctors ordered pain meds and the nurses started pumping them in me. Thankfully, between the nausea and pain meds I slept most of the time and only awoke from time to time in order to use the bathroom. I was on pain meds for several weeks before the tumor began to shrink.

I hated it, every bit of it—the sickness, the pain, the hospital stays, the constant medications, not going to school, and not being able to trap shoot and play football. I wanted the months that my treatment would take to go by and go by fast. I wanted my life back. To the best of everyone's ability, my family saw to it that I did everything exactly the way it was supposed to be done. I became a "good patient." I wanted to give myself the best shot I could of getting rid of my cancer.

Now you know why most of the activities in which I was involved and loved so much came to such an abrupt halt. I had cancer! Even after my treatment was complete, the surgeries and treatments, would likely leave my body unable to take the punishment of repeated hits in football and gun recoil. Because of the cancer, I am now missing the first two ribs on my right side. The cancer ate away the first and much of the second rib, the rest of it was removed during surgery. I was also told that radiation most of the time weakens the bones that are in and around the area of the body that is being radiated. So, not only am I missing bones, but the ones I have left in that area could now be weak. Would it really be worth the potential of getting seriously hurt? I did think I was pretty tough. After all, I finished my junior high football season at the top of my game and all that with a tumor in my chest the size of a cantaloupe compressing a third of my lung! We all agreed that decision could be made later.

I completed all my treatments right on schedule! None of my chemo treatments were delayed due to sickness or low counts. I recovered fully from surgery, breezed through radiation, and set a record with my stem cell transplant. I went into the hospital the day after Thanksgiving, began having heavy duty chemotherapy, got my cells which engrafted, and I was home before Christmas. I engrafted in just eight days! I wasn't expected to leave the transplant floor before February. Of course, I had to be careful. I had to stay away from crowds, and there was no eating out, but I was home! My treatment protocol was definitely not easy or quick! I hurt and was sicker than I had ever been in my life. But all my treatment went as planned with no recurrence or evidence of disease. It was the best case scenario, more likely than not I had an excellent chance of a cure. I started to resume my life. I was feeling stronger and my hair was growing back. It was darker and had a little wave to it. I was feeling much like I did before my diagnosis.

I returned to St. Jude every three months for full body scans and tests. My family and I would sit in that exam room, again, anxious and nervous for the results. After six months, and two checkups I was still clear of disease. That being the case, I got to have my central line removed! There was nothing to its removal, the surgery clinic doc just pulled it out. He put one hand on my chest and grabbed the end of the line with the other. He told me to take a deep breath then blow it out really hard, and when I did he jerked it out! Gone! Done! I went home and celebrated by taking a long, hot shower! Not a bath but a shower! It felt great! Another small piece of life back to normal.

I started thinking of returning to football and trap shooting. After all I had overcome, I knew if it was physically possible I could do it. I talked to my doctors and they set up some extra tests to measure the density of my bones. We even talked about coming up with some type of special padding to help distribute the pressure of an impact on my shoulder.

We returned to St. Jude for my nine month checkup. All the scans and tests had been done and we were waiting in the D Clinic waiting room to be called back for the results. Once again we were very nervous but a little more confident that the results would be good. While we were waiting, we tried to keep our minds occupied by cutting up and carrying on with a bunch of nonsense. We noticed someone who had a St. Jude badge taking a man and woman around showing them the blood donor and south waiting room. This is not an unusual occurrence. Tours are given of the hospital on a regular basis. But, this was an unusually small tour group and the guide was dressed up in a fancy suit (usually the guides are a little more casually dressed). Mom kept telling Dad that the man looked familiar, but she couldn't think who he was. The three of us kept staring, trying to figure out who this was. Finally, it came to us! It was Jeff Probst, the host of *Survivor*! To us that was big. Our whole family has been avid *Survivor* fans since the early days of the show.

Not being shy, we just went up and asked if he was actually who we thought he was. It was him! We talked to him for several minutes about the show and told him we had met several *Survivor* contestants including "Big Tom" from *Survivor Africa* and several from *Survivor Vanuatu*. He told us when we were ready to be on the show to let him know and he would make it happen! We had plans to take him up on his invitation! He was super nice and asked all about me and how I was doing. He signed a *Survivor* buff from the upcoming *Survivor China* show that was to air in the upcoming weeks. I had my picture made with him and I have both up on my wall at home. He wished me well and told me he was glad I was doing so good. He then continued on his tour of the hospital. I later learned he is a big supporter of St. Jude, helping raise large amounts of money for the hospital.

After meeting Jeff, we were called over the intercom to D Clinic. There we were met by Dr. McGregor. The news was not good. My cancer had returned in the form of a tumor in my left lung. It was about the size of a walnut and was the only spot they saw. More tests were set up and they all came back good. The plan was to remove the tumor and radiate both my lungs. Dr. McGregor knew that if my cancer was to come back, that it would likely pop up in the lungs. Again I was facing treatment and surgery. All I could think was, "Not again!"

I was so frustrated! I had worked so hard and had done everything like I was supposed to—exactly like I was supposed to. I was extra cautious and stayed away from people and places. I missed school, football games, activities, hunting seasons, and on many occasions, church. Sometimes, when I did go out around people I wore a mask. I was stared at and shied away from like I had the plague or something. I took every medication I was given without much complaint. I swelled from steroids so badly people would stare at me when they saw me. I was in the hospital every month and some of those stays were on holidays. I hurt in places I didn't even know I had, and I puked my guts out on a regular basis. I missed out on a year of my "normal" life. Why did it come back? But, again I did like I was told and again it was gone. This time for six months. Scans again and back again.

The third time it came back the doctors were not sure it was my Ewings because it grew so slowly.

Before doing any invasive treatment or surgery, they wanted to do a biopsy to determine exactly what the tumor was. The surgeon, Dr. Eubanks, who had done my chest re-section to remove the original tumor would do this biopsy because the tumor was in such a hard to reach place. The plan was to find out what it was while in surgery. If it was Ewing's Sarcoma, they would remove the tumor and put in a port so I could receive chemotherapy—again. Just like with the Hickman line, I was shown the device and shown where it would go in my body—the left side of my chest. That was just in case I would need it. There was still some doubt it was cancer.

Once again, I left my family and friends in the surgical waiting room and was taken to the operating room. Once again Dr. Eubanks performed the biopsy and surgery. After surgery I remember coming out of the fog of anesthesia. I reached up to my left side like you would when you put your hand over your heart to say the pledge of allegiance. I felt the bump under the skin and an incision close to it. No one had to tell me. I knew it was a subcutaneous port and it was there because once again the cancer was growing in my body.

The cancer has since come back three more times. The third time it came back in my brain. One evening, while watching the closing ceremonies of the Olympics, I started to get a bad headache so Mom gave me some *Tylenol*®. I sat back in my chair to relax and let it work while watching to see if they were going to put out the Olympic flame. Suddenly my head started hurting really bad and I started throwing up uncontrollably. Mom and Dad kept yelling frantically, "Jay, what's wrong?" The only thing I could get out was, "I don't know! Something's not right!" That was the last thing I remember until I woke up three days later in the LeBonheur Hospital Intensive Care Unit.

Without any warning, I had a tumor in my head that had grown in between check up scans. Actually, tumors are "faulty" cells our bodies fail to recognize and destroy. They also create for themselves a blood supply, but this too is faulty. The tumor's blood supply had burst causing what was similar to a stroke. I was first taken by ambulance to Gibson General Hospital in Trenton. The doctor and nurses in Trenton saved my life. They reacted quickly, giving me medications to keep the swelling down in my brain. Had it not been for them, I would have died that night. From there I was airlifted to Memphis LeBonheur Children's Hospital. Mom and Dad had to get to Memphis by car while I went by helicopter. They were so upset that our neighbor, Mr. Jeff Dickson, offered to drive them to Memphis so they would be sure to arrive safely. When they arrived, the doctors told them what was going on and that without surgery I would fade fast. They were also told that If I made it through surgery I probably would have a long recovery and more than likely I would never be back to what I was before. Obviously I made it through surgery and three days later I woke up. I knew everything and everyone. I picked up right where I had left off three days before. My first question was, "What happened," and my second one was, "Did they put that Olympic fire out?" The next day, I took my first steps, eight of them. I had beaten the odds and I give God the glory for it all!

I went through more chemo and brain radiation. The radiation to the brain continues to give me trouble. It has affected my appetite and causes me to have trouble controlling nausea. Because of these problems I have lost a lot of weight and much of my strength. I have even noticed some trouble with my memory. But I get by.

With yet another reoccurrence of disease I started and completed more chemotherapy. Again I had scans and again it was back. This time its return was worse. I had spots of disease throughout my body and for the first time the cancer was in my bone marrow. It was one of the darkest days of my life. Since this news, I have tried numerous experimental therapies from antibody therapy to Natural Killer Cell Infusion. In February 2010, Dr. McGregor told me that she felt she could no longer get rid of the cancer. She said that we could do some conventional chemotherapies with the hope of slowing it down and keeping it at bay. The hardest question I had yet to ask her but I did was, "How long?" With everyone in the room crying she told us..."Four to six months."

We returned home that afternoon and called all the family together and told them the news. It was a very emotional gathering.

I did decide to take conventional chemotherapy and so far it has been successful. The cancer is not gone, nor has it shrunk, but it is stable, no growth. As I write this it is now February of 2011, I continue to take therapy and enjoy life the best I can. I stay pretty active most of the time but wear out easily and when I get sick it takes me a long time to recover.

As of November of 2011, I have been a patient at St. Jude for six years. There I have made many special friends, some younger than me, some older. We share a bond that those who have not walked in our shoes can never understand. Some of those people are doing great and are living life to its fullest after beating cancer with a new appreciation for it. Some of those were too young while on treatment to ever remember what they had to go through. Now, they will only remember the occasional scans to check for disease. But some, unfortunately, have passed on. They fought hard and courageously but could not overcome the "beast." How bittersweet those memories are of the times we spent together.

My life will never return to the "normal" that it was before cancer invaded my body. Even if the cancer hadn't returned, life would have never been the same as before. Many things about life now seem to be better than before. My family and I now have a new "normal." Fitting this "new normal" in our life, it is just what we do without giving it another thought. Everyone has things in life they don't like to do but those things have to be done whether they like it or not. It is just different things for different people. The things in my life I don't like to do just happen to be chemo and being sick. I can look around and see that there is always someone who has a worse situation going on in life than I do. No one goes through life without challenges and problems. If this life was easy and carefree, we wouldn't see a need in seeking and living a life that is pleasing to God. But still, I do have my moments. I have adapted to what my life is now and in spite of it all I find that I am happy.

God has carried me and my family through the many tough times the past six years have brought us. My faith has grown tremendously and I know that if my journey on this earth ends sooner instead of later I will be in a much, much better place. For now, as Dad and I say, "Let's just try to keep it between the ditches."

6 Jay's Journey With Christ

The most important and beneficial journey in my life is my "Journey with Christ!" I guess to tell the whole story I would have to back up to 1987. That may sound strange since I was not born until January 21, 1992. But, continue to read and I will try to explain this wonderful journey.

I am very fortunate to have my parents. They met one another while attending Freed-Hardeman College (now Freed-Hardeman University). My dad graduated from West Carroll High School in May of 1986. My granddad talked him into going to college for one semester. After the first semester, December 1986, Dad packed up his stuff and headed home for good. My granddad said, "Son, get one year of college. That will help you in life." My granddad has since told me that he wanted Dad to stay at Freed-Hardeman to find a Christian wife. Dad, not knowing my granddad's intentions, finally agreed to go back and try one more semester. He made it to "spring break" and decided to quit. He was getting ready to leave school again and saw my mom playing foosball through a window at the student center. Dad told his friend, "Look at her, I would love to go out on a date with her." So dad stayed a little longer at FHU. However, Mom said, it took Dad about a month to get the nerve to ask her out on a date.

When he finally did get up the nerve to ask her out, Mom said "Yes" and so the story begins. Dad saw Mom for the first time in March of 1987. He asked her to marry him in May 1987. And, they were married August 15, 1987. Mom has said many times that she finished raising Dad (Mom is older, ha-ha) and she said she tried to straighten him out. Dad ended up changing his major to Bible and has been preaching for twenty-three years. My mom is a wonderful person and is a great strength for all of us. Mom and Dad always made sure Daniel and I was active in church and stressed to us that we should put God first in everything we do in life.

I will never forget the day I obeyed the Gospel of Christ. It was December 16, 2001 at the Independence church of Christ in Blue Goose, Tennessee. Many may be wondering what I did. The Bible teaches that by hearing God's word our faith is produced. Paul, an apostle of Jesus wrote, "So then faith cometh by hearing, and hearing by the word of God" (Roman 10:17). When I heard God's word, (I grew up listening to God's word but when I got old enough to understand the importance of it and the great need I had in my life for my Lord and Savior Jesus Christ) I began to ask more questions and I remember talking to Mom and Dad about what I needed to do to be saved. They told me what I want to tell everyone else, "Turn to God's word and not man for the answers." Not even my Dad and Mom could make it right for me to do something God did not say. We went to the book of Acts for more answers and understanding. In Acts chapter 2 we find some people who were listening to Peter preach. He had explained to them that they had rejected and crucified God's Son, Jesus Christ whom God had sent to save man from their sins. The Bible then says, "Now when they heard this, they were pricked in their heart, and said unto Peter and to the rest of the apostles, Men and brethren, what shall we do?" (Acts 2:37). I asked this question and so should everyone else. What must I do to have forgiveness of sins? What do I have to do to have the right relationship with God? What must I do to be a Christian? At this point I knew that I believed that Jesus was the Son of God and that He died on the cross for my sins. I knew the Bible said, "For God so loved the world that he gave his only begotten Son, that whosoever believeth in him should not perish, but have everlasting life" (John 3:16). When I heard God's Word and believed it, I still asked the question, "What must I do to be saved?" If you continue reading Acts 2, Peter answered that very question that had been asked in verse 37. The Scripture says, "Then Peter said unto them, Repent, and be baptized every one of you in the name of Jesus Christ for the remission of sins, and ye shall receive the gift of the Holy Ghost" (Acts 2:38).

As you read and study the Bible you will find that repentance is a change of our mind and our will. God requires us to repent. Paul wrote, "And the times of this ignorance God winked at; but now commandeth all men everywhere to repent: Because he hath appointed a day, in the which he will judge the world in righteousness by that man whom he hath ordained; whereof he hath given assurance unto all men, in that he hath raised him from the dead" (Acts 17:30-31). Jesus Himself said, "Repent or perish" (cf. Luke 13:3).

Having believed that Jesus is God's Son, and having repented of my sins, I knew there was still something else I need to do to be saved. Jesus had said, "He that believeth and is baptized shall be saved; but he that believeth not shall be damned" (Mark 16:16).

When I made up my mind about what I needed to do, I walked to the front of the church building during the invitation song (*Just as I Am*) and Dad (the preacher at the Independence church of Christ) had me sit down on the front pew. He asked me a few questions before we went any further. He asked if I understood what I was doing and why I was doing it. We stood up and Dad asked me if I believed that Jesus Christ was the Son of God. I answered, "Yes, I believe that Jesus Christ is the Son of God." That was the same confession made by a man, a eunuch from Ethiopia, I read about in the Book of Acts. The Bible says about him and Philip, the man who was teaching him; "And as they went on their way, they came to a certain water: and the eunuch said, See, here is water; what doth hinder me to be baptized? And Philip said, If thou believest with all thy heart, thou mayest. And he answered and said, I believe that Jesus Christ is the Son of God" (Acts 8:36-37).

After my confession I was baptized for the remission of my sins (Acts 2:38). After this the Lord added me to His church, His body, just as He did for those when the church was first established. The Bible says, "Praising God, and having favour with all the people. And the Lord added to the church daily such as should be saved" (Acts 2:47).

I will never forget that day as long as I live. It was really cold outside and the baptistery which was normally heated was not working that night. Thinking back about it, I will never forget my Dad's face as he went down in the water waiting on me to join him. He looked up at me and said, "Son, this is very cold." But I knew what I wanted and needed to do so I went down into the water and was baptized for the remission of my sins.

That was the greatest day of my life! Not only did I have forgiveness of my sins, but I also got in the right relationship with God my Father and Jesus my Savior. I gained a new home waiting for me in Heaven. We read in the Bible that one day Jesus will return for His people. He said, "Let not your heart be troubled: ye believe in God, believe also in me. In my Father's house are many mansions: if it were not so, I would have told you. I go to prepare a place for you. And if I go and prepare a place for you, I will come again, and receive you unto myself; that where I am, there ye may be also" (John 14:1-3). Just think! What would I be without Christ? Nothing!

Another thing that really helps me from day to day is that when I obeyed the Gospel of Christ, I got the promise of God's care. When I stop and think about it, I still have to say, WOW! That's amazing! God's care for me brings comfort to me and my family as I continue to battle against cancer. Jesus tells us just how much God looks out for us when He says, "No man can serve two masters: for either he will hate the one, and love the other; or else he will hold to the one, and despise the other. Ye cannot serve God and money. Therefore I say to you, Be not anxious for your life, what ye shall eat, or what ye shall drink; nor yet for your body, what ye shall put on. Is not the life more than food, and the body than raiment? Behold the fowls of the air: for they sow not, neither do they reap, nor gather into barns; yet your heavenly Father feedeth them. Are ye not much better than they? Which of you by being anxious can add one cubit to his stature? And why are ye anxious for raiment? Consider the lilies of the field, how they grow; they toil not, neither do they spin: And yet I say to you, That even Solomon in all his glory was not arrayed like one of these. Wherefore, if God so clotheth the grass of the field, which today is, and tomorrow is cast into the oven, *shall he* not much more *clothe* you, O ye of little faith? Therefore be not anxious, saying, What shall we eat? or, What shall we drink? or, With what shall we be clothed? (For after all these things do the Gentiles seek:) for your heavenly Father knoweth that ye have need of all these things. But seek ye first the kingdom of God, and his righteousness; and all these things shall be added to you. Therefore be not anxious for tomorrow: for tomorrow will be anxious for the things of itself. Sufficient to the day *is* its own evil" (Matthew 6:24-34).

With God's love, care, and promise to all who are obedient to His will I know He is watching over me and that regardless of when, if I stay faithful, I will have a wonderful home someday in heaven free of pain, sorrows, and sickness. I encourage all to study and put God first in your life.

Well, after I became a Christian my desire was to follow in Dad's footsteps and become a preacher. Mom always said I was "little Tim" and they both always encouraged me to be active in worship. A few years after I became a Christian, we moved our membership back to Trezevant so we could worship with all of our family. It was at the Trezevant congregation that Dad and my cousin Charlie taught a young men's training class where we spent time learning about the different parts of our worship to God. We would discuss singing, praying, partaking of the Lord's Supper, giving, and study or preaching during worship. We all took part in class and for a lack of a better way of putting it, we would practice in class and then every month or two our class would conduct/lead the worship on Sunday night. I remember how nervous I would get the night we would lead in front of the whole congregation, but, through all the encouragement of Charlie, my family, and the members of the church at Trezevant, each one of us in class continued to do more and more. A good friend of mine, Hayden McClain, who was also in the same class, always said that when we got older we would go hold Gospel meetings. We talked about how one of us could lead singing and the other could preach. As of yet, we have not done a Gospel meeting together, but we have conducted the services at Trezevant together many times. He would lead the singing and I would preach. I'd just like to add, Hayden is a great song leader now. He is as good as anyone I've ever heard lead singing.

Being active at church and trying to be a good, faithful Christian kept me out of some trouble. I know there were times when I wasn't the best example I should have been. But the older I get, the more I understand what Paul meant when he told Timothy to "Let no man despise thy youth; but be thou an example of the believers, in word, in conversation, in charity, in spirit, in faith, in purity" (1 Timothy 4:12). I have learned that even though you might be young, you can still be an influence and inspiration to those around you.

I guess I never considered my journey with Christ as closely as I have lately with the battle that I face every day with cancer. In February of 2010 when I received the news I had four to six months to live, that hit me and my family pretty hard. On our way home Mom and Dad called all our family and had them meet us at the church building at Trezevant. I wanted to tell them all at once and get it out of the way and not re-live it every day. It was a very emotional time for all. But I was thankful to get that behind me because it upsets me to see other people upset.

Mom, Dad, Daniel and I went home that evening, and we finished our night by talking about death, heaven, and what the Bible says about our finial journey. We finished the night with a long prayer with the four of us asking God to be with all of us every day that we have together.

Since that night, I know that I think about it and I'm sure that Mom and Dad spend a lot of time crying, praying, and thinking about me. But, we have tried to put it aside and live every day enjoying life, family, and friends. Not dwelling on impending death has helped me to drive forward and I'm still making big plans for the future.

I'm not sure when or where my journey with cancer will end. But one thing I do know. By the grace of God, and with all the understanding with which He assures us that we can know. **MY JOURNEY WITH CHRIST WILL NEVER END!** He is my Comfort, my Mediator, my King, my Elder Brother, my Friend, my Savior, and He is my All! Someday, I will live with Him forever.

7 Jay's Sermon Outlines

"For the preaching of the cross is to them that perish foolishness; but unto us which are saved it is the power of God...For after that in the wisdom of God the world by wisdom knew not God, it pleased God by the foolishness of preaching to save them that believe"
(1 Corinthians 1:18, 20)

On the following pages are a selection of my sermon outlines. Because of my health, many times I have been unable to attend Bible study and worship. During those times, I enjoyed studying my Bible by writing sermon outlines. I encourage everyone to take time to not only read through the outlines, but to also sit down with your Bible in your hand and look up the Scripture references. All of us need to be like those "noble Bereans" who "searched the scriptures daily, [to see] whether those things were so" (Acts 17:10)!

ALMOST PERSUADED

INTRODUCTION

I. What about that interesting word: "Almost"?

    A. Examples I've heard

        1. "We almost won the game!"
        2. "I almost won the lottery!"
        3. "I almost scored a goal!"
        4. "I almost made a 100 on my test!"
        5. One that happened to me as a football lineman on defense. "I almost intercepted the football!" (Maybe??? I would have scored a touchdown.)

    B. "I almost, but . . ."

II. Another interesting word: "Persuaded"

    A. Examples

        1. My parents: "Please let me have this new bicycle."
        2. Football team may be tired but one person says "Let's keep playing" and motivates others to continue

B. When I bought my first used truck, the salesman tried to convince (persuade) me that I really needed that particular truck

III. Let's look at the Bible and try to find a better meaning

DISCUSSION

I. *ALMOST PERSUADED*

A. King Agrippa (Acts 26:27-28)

1. He Believed
2. Almost persuaded to become a Christian

B. Not Ready to meet the Lord

II. *PERSUADED*

A. Philip and the Eunuch. (Acts 8:36-38)

1. The Eunuch believed
2. He was persuaded to become a Christian
3. He was getting ready to meet the Lord

CONCLUSION

I. Are you ready?
II. Paul was ready   2 Timothy 4:6-8
III. Do you need to get ready?
IV. Can we assist you in getting ready?

CAN WE HIDE FROM OUR SINS?

INTRODUCTION

I.   Text: Luke16:19-25
II. While growing up, my brother Daniel and I got into several mishaps. One I will never forget was the time we played tackle football in his room. To make a long story short, we hit the door and pushed the door knob through the wall. We tried to cover it up by using scotch tape and liquid paper. The next time Dad came into the room he asked; *"What happened to the wall?"* We said, we just opened the door and it knocked a hole in the wall. Dad asked several times so we would have an opportunity to tell the truth. But, we stuck to our story to the bitter end. He knew the truth and explained that we are better off telling the truth the first time because the truth always comes out.

DISCUSSION

I.   ***SOMETIMES WE MAY FEEL THAT WE CAN GET AWAY WITH OUR SINS***

   A. Romans 6:1
   B. Sin has a way of catching up with us

      1. No matter how hard we try to hide it, most of the time we will be discovered

2. Even if we can hide it from mom, dad, or others, the Lord knows

C. We must consider standing before the Lord with our sins
D. The children of Israel. Numbers 32:23

II. *WE MUST RID OURSELVES OF SINS BEFORE WE STAND BEFORE GOD ON JUDGMENT DAY*

A. Ephesians 1:7
B. Isaiah 59:1-2

III. *THE ONLY WAY TO DO THIS IS THROUGH THE POWER OF JESUS*

A. Reading and studying we can see Jesus' great *power* while on this earth and His great power He has now
B. We see Jesus had *compassion*
C. He has the power to forgive our sins

1. Matthew 9:1-8
2. Jesus has the power to heal us spiritually
3. Today He has the same power to heal our souls. To take our sins away
4. Luke 19:10 We find the reason Jesus came into this world

CONCLUSION

I. As a Christian, has sin taken over your life?

II. As you make your decision, remember, God wants you saved from sin

III. Are you trying to hide something from God today?

    A. There is no way!
    B. He already knows about it
    C. Be assured your sins *will* find you out

IV. When we obey God's will, (the Gospel) we receive God's power to save (Romans 1:16), and our sins are forgiven and remembered no more (Hebrews 10:17)

Dad and me before we preached at Sunday morning worship in 2010.

COUNT YOUR BLESSINGS

INTRODUCTION

I.   Text: Ephesians 1:3
II. What a Wonderful God is Ours!
III. God's help throughout the Bible

   A. Noah was told how to build the ark

      1. What to use to build it
      2. Everything he needed to survive the flood

         a. Genesis 6:22
         b. Genesis 9:1

   B. Daniel chapter 3

      1. Turn and explain the chapter (see especially verse 17)
      2. God took care of them because they stood on His side
      3. God loves and takes care of His people

IV. Our help today

   A. Romans 8:28
   B. Matthew 11:28
   C. 1 Corinthians 10:13

V.   Lead Statement: "We can count our blessings because…"

DISCUSSION

I. *JESUS CAME TO SAVE THE LOST*

    A. John 3:16-17
    B. Matthew 18:11
    C. Parable of lost sheep Luke 15:4-7
    D. Parable of lost coin Luke 15:8-10
    E. Parable of lost son Luke 15:11-32

II. *JESUS LEFT US AN EXAMPLE TO FOLLOW*

    A. Pick up cross and follow Jesus Matthew 16:24
    B. Carry Cross with Jesus Matthew 27:32

III. *HE HAS TOLD US HOW TO BE PREPARED*

    A. Paul had prepared himself 2 Timothy 4:6-8
    B. We need to be preparing to meet God Amos 4:12

        1. Jesus promised us a mansion if we go the right way John 14:1-4
        2. Which way? John 14:6

IV. *HE HAS TOLD US OF THE REWARD WAITING IN HEAVEN*

    A. Luke 6:23
    B. 1 Peter 1:3, 4

CONCLUSION

I. Have you counted your blessings lately?
II. If you are not a Christian you are missing so many spiritual blessings

   A. Hear the Word of God   Romans 10:17
   B. Do you believe that Jesus Christ is the Son of God? Acts 8:37
   C. Are you willing to repent of your sins? Luke 13:3
   D. Will you make that confession unto salvation? Romans 10:10
   E. Will you be baptized for the remission of your sins? Acts 2:38

III. Are you living a faithful Christian, life counting your many blessings? James 5:11

DESIRE

INTRODUCTION

I. I've tried to work crossword puzzles several times–
    I'm not very good
II. However, many words are very fascinating to me
III. For example, there is the word *"desire"* which
    means, "To long or hope for." (*Webster's Dictionary*)
IV. What is something you desire?
V. Let's take a closer look at this word and see how it
    can apply to us as Christians

    A. We should all desire to do good and be faithful
    Revelation 2:10

    B. We should all desire to work for God Nehemiah
    4:6

VI. Let's spell the word "desire" and try to find that
    deeper meaning for us as Christians

DISCUSSION

I. **<u>DETERMINE</u>**

    A. We must set our minds and be determined to
    Live faithful

    B. This will help us make sure we are in the right
    relationship with God 2 Peter 1:10

    C. Paul tells us to be "steadfast and unmovable" 1
    Corinthians 15:58

D. 2 Peter 3:17-18 tells us to be beware of being led to error. Verse 18 instructs us to grow in grace and knowledge

II. *ECHO*

A. Let each one of us live our lives echoing Jesus' words
B. Teaching others   Matthew 28:20
C. Loving others   John 15:12-19
D. Praying for others   John 17:9, 20

III. *SALVATION*

A. We must seek salvation at all cost
B. What do you seek most in this life?   Matthew 16:26
C. Put God first   Matthew 6:33
D. Paul said, Don't be ashamed of it!   Romans 1:16

IV. *INFLUENCE*

A. We should all have godly influences in our lives

1. Our elders   1 Timothy 3:7
2. Our members   Philippians 3:17; 2 Thessalonians 3:9
3. Our youth   1 Timothy 4:12

B. We should all be godly influences to others

V. *REPENT*

A. Change your life through repentance and confession of your sins
B. Repentance

    1. Perish Luke 13:3
    2. Change Acts 2:38
    3. Repent and be converted Acts 3:19
    4. Commanded Acts 17:30

C. Confession

    1. Confess and Pray James 5:16
    2. Confession unto salvation Romans 10:10
    3. Jesus will confess us to God Matthew 10:32
    4. He is faithful 1 John 1:9

VI. *ENCOURAGEMENT*

A. Our desire should be to encourage as many people as possible.
B. Encouragement can do much Hebrews 10:24
C. Others can see your happiness and it is contagious

    1. Your light shining will help other lights to shine Matthew 5:14-16
    2. Let people see that your life of encouragement is for God to have the Glory

CONCLUSION

I. What is your desire today?
II. Can we assist you in becoming a Christian?

    A. Faith, Repentance, Confession, Baptism
    B. Is your desire to come back to the Lord? James 5:16

III. Let's all be happy as Christians because we know that we have a King who is preparing us a "Home"

    A. John 14:1-3
    B. My desire is to live in that home some day
    C. What about You?
    D. It should show in our life!

FAITH

INTRODUCTION

I.   Nigra Falls

DISCUSSION

I.   *WHAT IS FAITH?*

   A. Hebrews 11:1
   B. Faith is the designation of an action that comes from a person's heart–called belief

      1. Romans 10:10
      2. Obedience comes from the heart
      3. What produces belief
      4. Romans 10:17
      5. Answer: "The Word of God"

   C. Faith itself is not salvation

      1. James 2:24
      2. James 2:26
      3. Faith in God and His Word leads us to seek salvation through obedience
      4. Matthew 6:33   "But seek ye **first** the kingdom of God"

II. *WHO HAD FAITH?*

A. Shadrach, Meshach, and Abednego

1. Daniel 3:16-25
2. Look at verse 28

a. "Then Nebuchadnezzar spake, and said, Blessed be the God of Shadrach, Meshach, and Abednego"
b. Their faith helped change other people

B. Faith blesses when man obeys   Hebrews 11:7
C. Many today   John 3:15

III. *WHY SHOULD WE HAVE FAITH?*

A. Eternal salvation is dependent on faith Hebrews 11:6
B. What does Faith do?   James 3:4-5

CONCLUSION

I. I think about myself and my faith. Where would I be without faith. The last four and half years I struggled but at the same time I prayed and believed that God would take care of me. As a matter of fact, four times when cancer hit me I beat it with God's help. Even as I stand before you today with the news we received a couple of weeks ago. (Given four to six months to live.) I still have faith and believe that God will take care of me no matter what happens or what the outcome may be. As a child of God our faith, trust, hope, and focus must be on Heaven

GOD'S FAMILY

INTRODUCTION

I.   Talk about the song "God's Family"
II. Explain personal meaning to you (Sung at Funeral of Granddaddy "Boat" Glen)

DISCUSSION

I. *EARTHLY FAMILY*

    A. Definition of a Family

        1. Example: Adam & Eve (Husband & Wife / Man & Woman)
        2. Children

    B. What should be found in a Family?

        1. Christian parents Ephesians 6:1
        2. A Daily Bible Study 2 Timothy 2:15
        3. Daily Prayer Luke 18:1
        4. Love for one another Colossians 3:18-21
        5. Faith in God Hebrews 11:1-6

    C. What is expected of each Family member

        1. The Husband/Father

            a. Assume position of head Ephesians 5:23
            b. Provide for the household 1 Timothy 5:8

    c. Love his wife Colossians 3:19
    d. Train children Ephesians 6:4

  2. The Wife/Mother

    a. Submit to husband Ephesians 5:22
    b. Love the husband Titus 2:4
    c. Love the children Titus 2:4
    d. Be keeper of the home Titus 2:5

  3. The Children

    a. Obey parents–this is right Ephesians 6:1
    b. Honor parents Ephesians 6:2

II. ***SPIRITUAL FAMILY***

A. Earthly family

  1. Common purpose of pleasing God
  2. Working together for a heavenly home

    a. Shared spirituality
    b. Shared goals
    c. Shared dreams
    d. Shared work in God's Kingdom
    e. Shared values

B. Our Local Congregation 1 Timothy 3:15

  1. Must submit to the authority of God Matthew 28:18-20

2. Must stand for the truth 1 Corinthians 15:58
3. Must have a mind to work Nehemiah 4:6

C. The Lord's church

1. Ephesians 5:23
2. Acts 2:47

III. *FAMILY REUNION*

A. Those before us 1 Thessalonians 4:16
B. Day of Judgment Matthew 25:31-46
C. Heaven Revelation 21:2-7; John 14:1-4

CONCLUSION

I. Challenge to each Family
II. Challenge to this congregation
III. Reward: Heaven our home

HOW TO BE A LIGHT

INTRODUCTION

I. Text: Matthew 5:14-16
II. When we think about light and darkness we know that light is good and darkness is evil

    A. So many things today are covered by darkness
    B. However this is nothing new
    C. Satan worked to cause Cain to kill Abel
    D. Satan worked hard on Job, but failed
    E. Satan got his grip on Judas who sold Jesus for 30 pieces of silver
    F. Over and over in the Bible we see many who gave in to darkness

III. We all can find people: friends, neighbors, co-workers, even family and possibly even yourself traveling through this world in total darkness
IV. We will look at "How To Be A Light!"

    A. But not just any regular light
    B. We are going to look at how to become a "bright light!"

DISCUSSION

I. *IF YOU WANT TO BE A BRIGHT LIGHT, THEN YOU MUST BE CLEAN!*

A. To become clean you must become a child of God–you must be washed!

  1. How do you get to the point where you are ready to be baptized?

     a. Hear Romans 10:17
     b. Believe Mark 16:16
     c. Repent Acts 2:38
     d. Confess Romans 10:10
     e. Now ready to be baptized 1 Peter 3:21

B. You must clean your cup and platter and keep it clean!

  1. What's more important cleaning the outside or the inside
  2. Matthew 23:25

C. Now if you have been washed and cleaned your plate and cup, you must keep your soul clean Revelation 2:10

II. *IF YOU WANT TO BE A BRIGHT LIGHT, THEN YOU MUST GET DRESSED!*

A. Paul tells us to put on the whole armor of God Ephesians 6:10-18
B. If we get dressed then we must build our faith

  1. What is faith? Hebrews 11:1
  2. Matthew 14:22-31

        a. Here we see Peter wanting to have great faith

        b. But, when the troubles got stronger his faith in the Lord got weaker and he began to sink

    3. Abraham took his son Isaac and because of his faith he was willing to sacrifice Isaac before the Lord Genesis 22:6-10.

C. When we get dressed and build our faith we will be ready and looking for the Lord

    1. Getting dressed includes our study of God's Holy Word to get us ready.

        a. 2 Timothy 2:15

        b. When we study we will be Ready to give an answer 1 Peter 3:15

    2. We should live our life looking for the Lord

        a. Titus 2:13-14

        b. 1 Thessalonians 4:16-17

III. ***IF YOU WANT TO BE A BRIGHT LIGHT, THEN YOU MUST TEACH OTHERS!***

A. Teaching others the Gospel is a command we must all follow

    1. Matthew 28:18-20
    2. Mark 16:15-16

B. We must teach others by our good example

    1. 1 Timothy 4:12
    2. Hebrews 10:24-2

CONCLUSION

I.   Have you become a child of God?
II. Have you been a good example in your faith?
III. Have you put your armor on and are you ready for the Lord to come?
IV. Will you commit yourself to be the "brightest light possible"?

I'M THANKFUL FOR MY FAMILY

I. *FATHER'S LOVE*

   A. Prodigal son Luke 15:11-32

II. *ATTITUDE TOWARD FAMILY*

   A. 1 Corinthians 1:10
   B. Ephesians 6:1-2 respect, honor

III. *MOTHER'S LOVE*

   A. Mary and Jesus John 19:26-27
   B. Special relationship with mother

IV. *"I" LAST*

   A. Selfishness 1 John 3:17

      1. Formula for JOY

         a. Jesus first in life

            1) Follow Jesus John 14:6
            2) Seek first kingdom of God Matthew 6:33
            3) Through Him we can be saved John 3:17

         b. Others second

        1) Show others love John 15:12
        2) Help others Galatians 6:2
        3) Go the second mile Matthew 5:41

    c. Yourself last

        1) Noah let go of the world and worldly ideas Genesis 6 & 7
        2) What are you going to profit? Mark 8:36-37
        3) The older brother Luke 15

  2. Mark Twain said: "Grief can take care of itself; but to get the full value from joy, you must have somebody to divide it with"

B. 1 John 3:11-12 teaches that one cannot find joy at the expense of others

V. *LOVE (1 CORINTHIANS 13)*

VI. *YOURSELF*

A. Your responsibility to God
B. Matthew 5:14-16 "you are a light"

CONCLUSION

I. All this points to the centering life of Christ and centering your life on Christ!

ONE WAY

INTRODUCTION

I. Have you ever been told there is just one way?

II. My dad told me about his time in the Army. While going through his training to be a paratrooper, he said many times he thought to himself, "What have I gotten myself in to this time?" Many times during the first two weeks of training (before boarding the plane for the third and final week) he would wonder, "How will I jump out of a perfectly good airplane?" He said the jumpmaster explained it to him while in the air before the jump. He said, "There is just one way down from here. You're going to jump. Nobody lands on this plane except the pilot and crew." I guess thanks to the jumpmaster Dad got his answer. You may be wondering what happened? Dad jumped!

III. This story reminds me of a few things about going to Heaven

DISCUSSION

I. ***THERE IS ONLY ONE WAY TO GET TO HEAVEN***

    A. Jesus said "I am the way, the truth, and the life; no man cometh unto the Father, but by me" John 14:6

    B. To reach the mark we need to grow spiritually

    C. What mark should we grow to?

1. We must be students of the Bible

    a. Prepare for Sunday School and Wednesday night Bible class
    b. Read the Bible through in a year and encourage your whole family to do it together

2. 2 Timothy 2:15 "Study to show thyself approved unto God, a workman that needeth not to be ashamed, rightly dividing the word of truth"

D. The more we study the better we can make the right choices in choosing a path that leads to heaven

II. *WE MUST CHOOSE THE RIGHT PATH*

A. Dad found the path to get back on the ground–jump out of the airplane!
B. What does it take to get to Heaven

1. The Lord talks about 2 paths in Matthew 7

    a. The first path leads to a wide gate–the entrance to destruction
    b. The Bible says many will find this Gate
    c. The second path leads to a narrow Gate–the entrance to life eternal/heaven
    d. The Bible says few will find this Gate

CONCLUSION

I. On the Day of Judgment will we have grown enough Spiritually to reach the mark and hear "Well done thy good and faithful servant" (Matthew 25:21, 23) or will we fall short and hear "depart from me" (Matthew 25:41)

II. Even at a young age we need to be working toward Heaven

   A. Put God and His kingdom first Matthew 6:33
   B. Let your "light shine" Matthew 5:16
   C. Be a good "example" 1 Timothy 4:12

III. We must start on our right path by growing enough to be Christians–"Faithful Christians!"

REMOTE
Devotional for Youth

INTRODUCTION

I. Show a remote control
II. Talk about the remote control
III. How do we apply a remote control to our life?

DISCUSSION

I. *RANGE*

    A. Closeness
    B. James 4:8

II. *ENERGIZE*

    A. Power
    B. Romans 1:16

III. *MUTE*

    A. Turn off the wrong sounds
    B. Listen to the right ones 2 Timothy 3:16-17

IV. *OPPORTUNITIES*

    A. 2 Timothy 2:15
    B. Galatians 6:10

V. **_TIME_**

    A. Time your parents let you watch
    B. Matthew 16:24-26

VI. **_EVERY TIME_**

    A. Jesus is there for you every time
    B. 1 Corinthians 10:13

CONCLUSION

I. Remembering the REMOTE can help us to live a more faithful Christian life
II. Are you under remote control?

THE LION KING

INTRODUCTION

I. We all have favorite television shows and movies

    A. When I was younger, my family and I watched most all the Disney movies–*Hercules, Jungle Book, Toy Story*
    B. But, one of my favorites was/is *The Lion King*
    C. Not only did I have the movie, I had shirts, caps, house shoes, shoes, games, toys, bed sheets, comforter, and many other things all with the Lion King displayed

II. Explain the movie, *The Lion King*

    A. Song: "The Circle of Life"
    B. Characters–Simba, Pumbaa, Timon, Mufasa, Scar
    C. Where did the King stand–"Pride Rock"
    D. Pumbaa and Timon favorite saying: "Hakuna Matta" which means "no worries"

III. Simba, started out in the movie saying, "I just can't wait to be King! Nobody saying do this or do that!"

    A. Not sure if he was interested in being successful for the right reason, or just interested in being on top–Maybe he wanted to be the greatest
    B. Remember Jesus' teaching in Mark 9:35?

IV. Most everyone wants to succeed in life

A. We want to make something of ourselves
B. Be successful!

V. What is the "Key to Success?"

    A. We all know an education is important in Life
    B. Some have said that it is the "key to success"
    C. And surely, if education is the key to success in life, knowledge and education on spiritual matters is the most important key

VI. How do we gain the knowledge and get the education for spiritual success?

DISCUSSION

I. *WATCH OUR DAILY CONDUCT IF WE WANT TO BE SUCCESSFUL CHRISTIANS*

    A. No man can be wrong with man and right with God Matthew 5:23-24
    B. Follow God's Word James 1:22
    C. Mr. Rogers "good neighbor"
    D. The Good Samaritan Luke 10:30-36

II. *DO YOU REALLY WANT TO BECOME A STRONG, FAITHFUL CHRISTIAN?*

    A. Four Good rules:

        1. Study your Bible daily

      a. 1 Peter 2:2
      b. 2 Timothy 2:15

2. Pray every day

      a. Matthew 7:7
      b. James 5:16

3. Attend all the services of the church

      a. Hebrews 10:25
      b. "Do I have to" is a very dangerous attitude
      c. We have the privilege; we need the spiritual food

4. Give liberally of time, talents, and means

      a. 1 Corinthians 16:2
      b. Invest in Heaven. Where your treasure is, there will your heart be

B. These can help us to grow in strength

III. *DEFINITION OF A CHRISTIAN*

A. These may sound simple, but I feel they are very important to our daily conduct and living a Christian life
B. CHRISTIAN

1. C–One's life should be Christ centered
2. H–One should have a strong Home life
3. R–One should be Ready to serve
4. I–One should be an Influence to others
5. S–One should be Strong in the faith
6. T–One should be Trustworthy
7. I–One should be Involved
8. A–One should be Aware of Christian duties
9. N–One is a New Creature

CONCLUSION

I. Back to the movie–Mufasa (Simba's Dad) wanted the very best for his son

    A. The Prodigal Son's Father

        1. Father had the younger son in future plans

            a. His inheritance Luke 15:12
            b. His happiness Luke 15:12

        2. Father very concerned about younger son

            a. Watching and waiting Luke 15:20
            b. Compassion and love Luke 15:20

        3. Father overjoyed with his return

            a. Robe, ring and shoes Luke 15:22
            b. Plans for welcome home meal Luke 15:23

  c. Happiness and welcome home party Luke 15:25

  d. Full of forgiveness and thanksgiving for his return Luke 15:32

 4. Father wanted very best for both his sons

II. God wants the very best for us

 A. God has promised us a wonderful place to spend eternity, if we are faithful to Him

  1. John 14:1-3
  2. 1 Thessalonians 4:13-17
  3. Revelation 21:2-7

 B. This is the whole purpose for sending Christ

  1. John 3:16-17
  2. John 14:15
  3. James 4:8

THERE IS POWER IN THE BLOOD

INTRODUCTION

I. In my battle against cancer I know how important blood really is. I now have to receive blood at least once a week. Without the blood transfusions I will become very weak. I can't help but think about the "Power in the Blood of Christ" that helps keep me from becoming weak as a Christian.

II. Many times in life we all become weak: Physically, mentally, emotionally, or even spiritually. But the power in Jesus' precious blood never runs out or becomes weak.

III. Let's take a closer look at the Power found in the blood

DISCUSSION

I. *POWER OF SIN*

A. Sin leads to death   Romans 6:23
B. Sinful communications   1 Corinthians 15:33
C. Sin leads to destruction   Matthew 7:21-23

II. *POWER OF THE BLOOD*

A. On the Cross

1. Total Darkness Matthew 27:45
2. Earthquake Matthew 27:51
3. Graves Open Matthew 27:52

4. "Truly this was the Son of God" Matthew 27:54

B. Wash Away Sins

1. Acts 22:16
2. Ephesians 1:7
3. Colossians 1:14

C. Remembrance

1. His death

   a. Suffering, shame, and humiliation Isaiah 53:1-10 and Philippians 2:5-10
   b. Demonstration–God's love Romans 5:8

2. God has provided the means of remembering the death of Christ

   a. The New Testament record
   b. The plan of salvation emphasizes it Romans 6:1-6

3. Our Worship

   a. Songs emphasize the great fact
   b. The Lord's Supper is a memorial to the fact of Christ's death Luke 22:19-20; 1 Corinthians 11:23-29

CONCLUSION

I. Are you weak today?

II. Maybe you need a blood transfusion

III. Let the Blood of Christ give you the strength today to overcome the obstacles in your life

    A. There is Power in the Blood

    B. "I can do all things through Christ who strengtheneth me" Philippians 4:13

THERE'S A GREAT DAY COMING

INTRODUCTION

I.   We all have "favorite days" and "worst days"

A.   My "favorite days"

1.   The day I was baptized (December 16, 2001)
2.   The day I caught my first fish
3.   The day my trap shooting team won forth in the state
4.   Day my football jersey was retired at West Carroll High School
5.   Day I graduated from High School

B.   My "worst days"

1.   The day my granddaddy passed away
2.   The day I found out I had cancer

C.   What about for you?

III. We all have "favorite days," "worst days," and days we are dreading or looking forward to
IV. For us as Christians we sing a song: "There's A Great Day Coming"

DISCUSSION

I.   *GREAT DAY COMING   (MATTHEW 7:13-14)*

A. Saints
B. Sinners
C. Parted right and left

II. *BRIGHT DAY COMING*

A. Those who are obedient (Mark 16:16)
B. Saints: "Well done" (Matthew 25:21)
C. Heaven our Home

    1. Rest

        a. Matthew 11:28
        b. Revelation 14:13
        c. Rest from sin and temptation awaits us there Revelation 21:27
        d. Rest from all the violence and wickedness of society

    2. Restoration

        a. Renewal of association with God our Father Revelation. 21:3
        b. Worn bodies completely restored 2 Corinthians 4:16 - 5:1; Philippians 3:21

    3. Reserved for the faithful

        a. Revelation 21:25
        b. 1 Peter 1:4
        c. 2 Timothy 4:8

III. *SAD DAY COMING (MATTHEW 7:21-23)*

A. Sad day for who?

    1. The devil and his angels   Matthew 25:41
    2. Those who don't obey Gospel   2 Thessalonians 1:7-9
    3. Unfaithful members   2 Peter 2:20
    4. Names not written   Revelation 20:15
    5. Some specific classes named   Revelation 21:8; Galatians 5:19, 21

B. Sinners: "Depart, I know you not"

CONCLUSION

I. What should you do to make it a Bright Day?

A. No sin can enter Heaven   1 John 1:5-10
B. No one can get there unless he

    1. Believes   Hebrews 11:6; Acts 16:31
    2. Repents   Luke 13:3; Acts 17:30
    3. Confess Christ Matthew 10:32; Romans 10:10
    4. Baptized   Galatians 3:26-27; Romans 6:3-4; 1 Peter 3:21
    5. Is faithful   Revelation 2:10; 2 Peter 1:10; 1 Corinthians 15:58

WHEN WE ALL GET TO HEAVEN

INTRODUCTION

I. Most children have made at least one of these statements: "How much further?" "Are we there yet?" or "When will we be there?"
II. Let's answer the question: "What are we doing to get there?"

DISCUSSION

I. *WE'RE SINGING (EPHESIANS 5:19)*

    A. Singing about the Love of Jesus John 15:12-13
    B. Singing about Mercy and Grace
    C. Singing about our mansion in Heaven   John 14:1-3

II. *WE'RE WALKING (1 JOHN 1:7)*

    A. Walking as Pilgrims

        1. Hebrews 11:13
        2. 1 Peter 2:11

    B. One Day our Travel will end

        1. Let our traveling end with the confidence that Paul had   2 Timothy 4:6-8
        2. Ecclesiastes 7:8 "Better is the end of a thing than the beginning thereof..."

    3. Philippians 1:21

III. *WE'RE SERVING*

  A. We Must be True and Faithful

    1. 1 Corinthians 10:13
    2. Hebrews 10:22

  B. Everyday Service

    1. Acts 26:7 ". . . earnestly serving [God] day and night"
    2. Acts 2:41-47

  C. We're serving to be with Him in Glory

    1. 1 Thessalonians 4:13-18
    2. Matthew 25:34-40

CONCLUSION

I. Where are you going?
II. Jerry Clower: "Where will you be when you get where your going?"

WHERE COULD I GO?

INTRODUCTION

I. What do you do when faced with a real big decision?

II. How do you finally make up your mind what to do?

DISCUSSION

I. *MAKING A GOOD CHOICE WHEN FACED WITH A BIG DECISION*

    A. Whether or not to obey God   John 14:6

    B. To Remain Faithful   John 6:66-68

II. *TWO QUESTIONS–LET'S ANSWER TOGETHER*

    A. To whom could we Go?

        1. Many people follow what the majority believes

        2. Remember Noah +7 vs. everyone else

        3. Many people follow what feels good, the world, Satan/Devil

        4. Matthew 7:13-14

    B. To whom should we Go?

        1. John 6:68

        2. Remember our other verse   John 14:6

CONCLUSION

I.   Sometimes we lose our way–we find ourselves lost
II. Noah's story–Most thought "Go where I want"
III. Noah and family followed God
IV. Find your way–Jesus is the Way and He has the words of eternal life

8 Jay's Articles

On the following pages are a few of the articles I have written. Like the sermon outlines, I hope you will read them and learn the lessons I am trying to teach.

Keep It Between the Ditches

When I was growing up my dad would sometimes use the saying, "Keep it between the ditches." He said it when something was going wrong in our lives, or when things seemed to be getting wild or out of control. I always knew what he meant, and somehow it always helped. It would cause me to simply slow down and think through whatever situation I was in.

As you can imagine, when we were told I had cancer, my whole family and I were really upset. It was overwhelming when the doctors told us the treatment, the odds, and the path I would have to travel to give myself the best chance of survival. I was 13 years old and I had a lot of other plans for my life. These plans didn't include losing my hair, being sick to my stomach all the time, and spending my teenage years in and out of the hospital. But as you may already have guessed, we used our saying! If we wanted the end result, (defeating cancer), then we must travel this path and "keep it between the ditches!" I have always tried to "keep it between the ditches" even though my cancer would go away and then come back in a different spot.

In February 2010, Dr. Lisa McGregor came in my room after I had completed all my tests and scans. She had a very sad look on her face. She told me my cancer was back yet again, and it had spread throughout my body. To make the news worse, she said I had gone through all the treatments known to help my cancer and we had no others to try. She told me she would begin chemo again to try to slow down the growth and spread of my cancer.

Before I went any further, I asked a question I never dreamed I would have to ask. I said, "How long do you think I have?" What she said hurt my family and me so very badly. We couldn't control our emotions for quite some time. She said, "Jay, you have four to six months to live if you take more treatment." Mom always says that I don't have "give up" or "quit" in me. So, I told Mom and Dad: "This is our new path and let's "keep it between the ditches." As I write this article I am approaching my sixth month. I'm struggling with my health but I continue on my course.

As we travel through our life, longing for our home in heaven we have to keep on our path. Jesus said we get to choose which path to travel when He said: *"Enter ye in at the strait gate: for wide is the gate, and broad is the way, that leadeth to destruction, and many there be which go in thereat: Because strait is the gate, and narrow is the way, which leadeth unto life, and few there be that find it"*(Matthew 7:13-14). Unfortunately, the wide path is the one most commonly traveled. Though it may be more difficult, we ought to strive to "keep it between the ditches" of the narrow way that leads to Heaven. Even when we feel we are in a hard, or even losing battle, we need to "keep it between these ditches."

I sometimes wonder what to do and which way to go now. But I always go back to the only answer I have, and that answer is found in God's Word. Jesus is the answer and He is the **right way** to go. John tells us, *"Jesus saith to him, I am the way, and the truth, and the life: no man cometh to the Father, but by me"* (John 14:6). We must want to get to our Father in heaven. We know through His teaching what a wonderful place Heaven must be.

I hope and pray that we can all learn to "keep our lives between the ditches of the narrow path."

If It Ain't Broke, Don't Fix It!

My granddaddy, J.T. Rogers, is a really good mechanic. He is especially good at working on small engines. When my dad was younger, he always wanted to be a mechanic. He heard my granddad make a statement one time that he could put a small engine together that he found torn apart with all the parts in different buckets.

Being young, and not really understanding the difficulty of working on a motor, my dad went to the barn and found a lawnmower. This mower did not need any major repairs. As a matter of fact, it was running good up until this point. Well, my dad found some empty buckets and tools, and he started taking parts off the motor and putting them into the buckets. It wasn't long until he had this lawnmower engine torn apart. You guessed it. When he started putting it back together, he couldn't remember which parts went where! He put everything back as best he could, and then left it not saying anything to his dad.

Have you ever known someone who couldn't leave well enough alone? Or, maybe they try to fix or change something that isn't broken. This happens quite often. It is not just with kids with lawnmowers. It happens with the Bible and the church. Some people just can't leave things alone. They try to fix things that are not broken.

The Bible warns us about trying to change or "fix" God's words. *"For I testify to every man that heareth the words of the prophecy of this book, If any man shall add to these things, God shall add to him the plagues that are written in this book: And if any man shall take away from the words of the book of this prophecy, God shall take away his part out of the book of life, and out of the holy city, and [from] the things which are written in this book"* (Revelation 22:18-19). The Lord has left us a plan. It is His plan of salvation.

First, we must **hear** the word of God. Paul wrote, *"So then faith [cometh] by hearing, and hearing by the word of God"* (Romans 10:17). After we have heard the word, we must **believe** what it says. Jesus said, *"For God so loved the world, that he gave his only begotten Son,* *that whoever believeth in him should not perish, but have everlasting life"* (John 3:16). Then Peter tells us we must **repent** of our sins: *"Then Peter said to them, Repent ye, and each one of you be baptized in the name of Jesus Christ for the remission of sins, and ye shall receive the gift of the Holy Spirit"* (Acts 2:38). God's plan also includes the great **confession** that we read about when the Eunuch from Ethiopia said *"...I believe that Jesus Christ is the Son of God"* (Acts 8:37). It is the same confession Paul was talking about when he wrote, *"For with the heart man believeth unto righteousness; and with the mouth confession is made unto salvation"* (Romans 10:10). Just like Philip taught the eunuch, after we make that great confession we can have our sins washed away through baptism. The text in Acts continues, *"And he commanded the chariot to stand still: and they both went down into the water, both Philip and the eunuch; and he baptized him"* (Acts 8:38). Jesus said, *"He that believeth and is baptized shall be saved; but he that believeth not shall be damned"* (Mark 16:16). After we complete our obedience through baptism, we must spend the rest of our life faithful to God for the Scriptures say, *"...be thou faithful to death, and I will give thee a crown of life"* (Revelation 2:10).

As we have already noted, the Lord tells us in His word what we must do to be saved. But what if we don't follow God's plan? Can we expect to be saved and have a home in heaven if we choose not to follow the narrow path? Jesus said, *"Enter ye in at the narrow gate: for wide is the gate, and broad is the way, that leadeth to destruction, and many there are who go in by it: Because small is the gate, and narrow is the way, which leadeth to life, and few there are that find it"* (Matthew 7:13-14). If Noah had made the ark out of oak wood do you think the ark would have floated and Noah and his family would have been saved from the flood? The answer is **no!** The Lord told Noah exactly how to build the ark (Genesis 6:14-16). The Bible tells us, *"Thus did Noah; according to all that God commanded him, so did he"* (Genesis 6:22). Had he used oak instead of gopher wood, he would not have obeyed God nor could he have expected His blessing. There are other examples in the Bible such as: Shadrach, Meshach, and Abednego (Daniel 3), and many others we read about in Hebrews 11 that were counted among the faithful because of their obedience.

An example of not doing what the Lord said is found in Genesis 19. Two angels came to tell Lot the Lord was going to destroy Sodom and Gomorrah. He was told: *"...Escape for thy life; look not behind thee, neither stay thou in all the plain; escape to the mountain, lest thou be consumed"* (Genesis 19:17). Later, when Lot and his family were fleeing, his wife looked back and she was turned into a pillar of salt. If she had done as God instructed, she would not have turned into a pillar of salt.

After God created Adam, the Bible says, *"And the LORD God commanded the man, saying, Of every tree of the garden thou mayest freely eat: But of the tree of the knowledge of good and evil, thou shalt not eat of it: for in the day that thou eatest of it thou shalt surely die."* (Genesis 2:16-17). Later, Eve was tempted by Satan and ate of that tree (Genesis 3:1-5). The Bible tells us, *"And when the woman saw that the tree was good for food, and that it was pleasant to the eyes, and a tree to be desired to make one wise, she took of its fruit, and ate, and gave also to her husband with her; and he ate. And the eyes of them both were opened, and they knew that they were naked; and they sewed fig leaves together, and made for themselves aprons"* (Genesis 3:6-7). Adam and Eve disobeyed the Lord.

As long as we have the right to choose which path to travel, we will always have people who want to fix things that are not broken. We will always have young children trying to be like their parents and tear apart lawnmowers. But, we must choose to follow God's plan the way He has laid it out. It is perfect. It is perfect for us. It is fixed. It ain't broke.

Some people follow God and are counted among the faithful. Some people disobey the Lord. Which choice will you make?

Walk This Way

How are you walking? I hope you are walking as a faithful Christian. If so, let us continue in the path that "leads unto life" (Matthew 7:13-14). Let us go forward with the attitude of rejoicing because of our Lord and Savior Jesus Christ. Our prayer should be that this attitude will cause our light to shine even brighter than it has ever shined before(Matthew 5:14-16).

As Christians we are not perfect, but we are forgiven, blessed, and hopeful! Let's commit ourselves (everyone) to doing even more for the Lord's body—

His church! Doing more must include walking more and/or further as Christians.

Jesus says *"And whosoever shall compel thee to go a mile, go with him twain."* (Matthew 5:41). He is teaching that one should be willing to give more than that which is normally expected of him. The second mile is the real test of Christianity, it demands that one go all the way with the Lord (see John 14:6).

What is the purpose of the "second Mile"? I believe that as Christians we should go beyond the sinner and even the good moral person in our duty to others and the Lord. We should show the world the difference in the world and Christianity and between being of the world or being in Christ. I challenge each of us to express the real spirit of Christianity.

"The second mile." Christ is at the end of that mile and it is where real Christianity begins.

Let's Slow Down and Rethink This!

It seems like everything changes very fast in our world today. As a matter of fact, even we are moving faster. We have so many things to do and so many places to go, we are going, going, and going some more. And usually, this is at a very fast pace. Instead of sitting down and eating a meal, we can, in only a minute or two, order what we want, drive to a window pay for and pick up our food, and then eat it while driving down the road.

Generally, we are people who are in a hurry to get where we are going. (Normally running late!) Because we are so busy, we sometimes find ourselves leaving some things undone. Often, we leave out our family time and our time we should be devoting to God.

Wouldn't it be nice to start a "new religion" that would allow us to do things the way we wanted, when we wanted, and what we wanted in our worship of God? This would probably fit our lifestyle better, but starting a "new religion" or a "church" is not possible and still be in the right relationship with God. God, through His Word (The Bible), has instructed us how He wants us to worship and live. Although the world is changing daily and we are getting more high tech, our Lord and Savior Jesus Christ remains, *"...the same yesterday, and today, and forever"* (Hebrew 13:8).

Other verses in the Word of God tell us we should not be changing God's way. Notice what Paul told Timothy: in, *"All scripture is given by inspiration of God, and is profitable for doctrine, for reproof, for correction, for instruction in righteousness: That the man of God may be perfect, thoroughly furnished unto all good works"* (2 Timothy 3:16-17). The Bible teaches the Scriptures are complete and the law of the Lord is perfect when the Psalmist wrote, *"The law of the LORD is perfect, converting the soul: the testimony of the LORD is sure, making wise the simple"* (Psalms 19:7). Because of all this, there is no room for change. Christ is unchanging and is the very heart of Christianity.

Also, notice that Paul wrote, *"Moreover, brethren, I declare unto you the gospel which I preached unto you, which also ye have received, and wherein ye stand; By which also ye are saved, if ye keep in memory what I preached unto you, unless ye have believed in vain. For I delivered unto you first of all that which I also received, how that Christ died for our sins according to the scriptures; And that he was buried, and that he rose again the third day according to the scriptures:"* (1 Corinthians 15:1-4). The facts of the Gospel of Christ never change, nor do the facts to be believed—the *death, burial, resurrection.*

Do we need to start a new religion? The answer to this is most definitely, **no**! If we will continue to preach, teach, and live by God's Holy Word we will have the hope of Heaven. Paul wrote, *"But though we, or an angel from heaven, preach any other gospel unto you than that which we have preached unto you, let him be accursed. As we said before, so say I now again, If any man preach any other gospel unto you than that ye have received, let him be accursed"* (Galatians 1:8-9). We have the Gospel of Christ. The Gospel of Christ will solve every problem of the world if we will study and apply it to our lives.

We shouldn't start a new religion, nor should we be looking for one. We shouldn't be looking for change in God's Word. The Word of God is complete, perfect and shall not pass away. Jesus said, *"Heaven and earth shall pass away, but my words shall not pass away"* (Matthew 24:35). Instead of looking for a change or something new we should do what Paul said when he wrote, *"my beloved brethren, be ye stedfast, unmoveable, always abounding in the work of the Lord, forasmuch as ye know that your labour is not in vain in the Lord"* (1 Corinthians 15:58).

My prayer is that we can all slow our lives down, show love to our family, friends, neighbors, fellow Christians and Father in Heaven. Let's slow down to the point that we spend needed time in God's Word. The Bible says, *"Study to show thyself approved to God, a workman that needeth not to be ashamed, rightly dividing the word of Truth"* (2 Timothy 2:15). If we spend time in study we will know we must follow God's teaching, His plan for worship, and His plan of salvation.

We can also learn to be content. Paul knew how to be content. He spent time in prison for living a Christian life and he learned to be content. He wrote, *"Not that I speak in respect of want: for I have learned, in whatever state I am, [with that] to be content"* (Philippians 4:11). With knowledge we will be happy with "just living a Christian life" and not looking for something more convenient.

The Challenge

The challenge before us is simple to explain but harder to carry out. The goal before us is to preach, teach, and spread the Gospel to everyone. Our goal is to put forth an honest effort to grow the church. I believe these two go hand and hand. We are to "go and teach all nations, baptizing them in the name of the Father, and of the Son, and of the Holy Ghost: . . ." (Matthew 28:19-20) and "Go into all the world, and preach the gospel to every creature. He that believeth and is baptized shall be saved; . . ." (Mark 16:15-16). The Bible teaches us when people truly believe and obey then souls will be added to the Lord's church (Acts 2:47). This is how people can rejoice (Acts 8:39) because Jesus is the "Savior of the body" (Ephesians 5:23).

Precious souls need to be won to Christ so they can be added to the body of Christ. Let's all commit to working for this **goal**.

Here's a little something to help us get started in reaching our GOAL.

1. Who can I ask to come?
   Relatives:
   Classmates:
   Neighbors:
   Special Friends:
2. Who do I have contact with daily (who's not listed above)?
3. Do I pray for my friends daily?
4. Have I shared the Gospel with my friends?
5. Have I invited my friends to attend worship with me?
6. Do I know the spiritual needs of my friends?
7. Do I live the Christian life before my friends?
8. Choose two friends from the above list and begin praying specifically for them and then invite them to come to our Worship Services.

This really could be "a day your friend could remember for eternity" Jesus said, "Greater love hath no man than this, that a man lay down his life for his friends" (John 15:13).

Study Questions

1. What does the word "church" mean?
2. Where is the church first mentioned in the New Testament?
3. Who promised to build the church?
4. In what year did the church begin?
5. In what city did the church begin?
6. On what day did the church begin?
7. Who preached a great sermon that day?
8. How many people were added to the church that day?
9. The church is also call the _____ of Christ. (Ephesians 1:22-23)
10. Who is the head of the church? (Ephesians 5:23)
11. Who gave himself for the church? (Ephesians 5:25)
12. Who loved the church? (Ephesians 5:25)
13. With what was the church purchased? (Acts 20:28)
14. The church is subject to whom? (Ephesians 5:24)
15. Christ is the savior of what? (Ephesians 5:23)
16. What is the body? (Colossians 1:24)
17. The church is not the building but the _____ .
18. There are how many spiritual bodies? (Ephesians 4:4)
19. What is the pillar and ground of the truth?
20. The church was founded by what scriptural builder.

9 About Jay

On the next few pages you will be reading some thoughts others have to share about Jay. It should already be apparent to the readers of this book that Jay is a marvelous example of a young man whose character is most worthy of imitation. The words you are about to read will continue to attest to that fact. Indeed, nothing but good things are said about him on the following pages, but then again, there is not much else anyone could say about Jay.

It has been my privilege to know Jay Rogers almost from the day he was born. Though he is a bit younger than my own children, he and his brother, Daniel, did occasionally spend time visiting and playing with them. If you have ever spent time watching children as they play, you know you can learn a lot about their nature by the way they interact with others. And though all children usually have a little mischief in them, it was always evident that Jay was a good kid!

But, as I have watched him grow over the years, it has become more apparent to me that Jay Rogers is more than just a "good kid." He has grown into a fine young Christian man whose character and courage inspires all who are blessed with the opportunity to have even a momentary association with him. Whether it be on the athletic field, on a hunting trip, in a church building, or in a life-altering brawl with a fiendish foe called cancer, he has always proven himself to be a person of determination, honor, and integrity.

If you have ever had the opportunity to have a conversation with Jay, you have witnessed his kind, humble, and unassuming demeanor. His love for his family, for his friends, and especially for his God is unmistakable. Though he has trophies to display as a result of his athletic achievements and his adventurous hunts, his family, his friends, and his God are far more cherished by him.

To me, Jay is reminiscent of the Bible character, Job, of which the Bible says, "...that man was blameless and upright, and one who feared God and shunned evil" (Job 1:1, NKJV). If you know the story of Job, you know he got knocked around pretty hard in life. We could say the same about Jay. His life has seen more than its share of struggles for someone so young. When things looked as though they could get no worse, often they did. He has kept getting up to fight one more round, only to get knocked down again. On more than one occasion when it seemed as though he was going to cross the finish line and beat his disease, cancer would stick out it's foot and trip him. But, like Job, Jay has held fast to his integrity (Job 2:3) and faith in God. His perseverance has been both extraordinary and inspirational.

Like so many, our prayers keep going up to the Father in Heaven for Jay, Tim, Wendy, Daniel, and all his family. Yes, we ask Him to bless Jay with improved health and more time to spend here in this life. But in those prayers we also thank God for allowing us the great privilege of knowing and being blessed by the example of a courageous young man named Jay Rogers.

Mark Howell
Midway church of Christ
Jasper, Alabama

In this book you have been introduced to an extraordinary young man whose childhood journey over the last seven years has taken him down roads most adults never travel. And along the way he has learned some things about life, faith, and resilience that many adults never learn, either.

I have known Jay since the earliest hours of his journey. He has blessed my life in ways too numerous to list, but I want to recall a few that seem to me to be important.

- At each juncture of his struggle against childhood cancer, Jay has kept his eyes open for the ways God is blessing him. He has been wise in understanding that the human experiences of worry and sadness do not mean that God's love and grace have been a failure. To the contrary, at those times when the news has not been good, Jay's commitment to live in the presence of the living Christ has grown all the stronger.

- Early on, Jay developed the habit of hanging a pillowcase over his IV stand to hide the bags of chemotherapy that coursed through plastic lines into his body. By doing this, Jay seemed to be saying "I will not be defined by my illness. I may have to take this medicine, but I don't have to dwell on it." There is so little that a young adolescent receiving cancer treatment can control; Jay found something he could control and asserted his power. In this small gesture, and many others, Jay witnessed to his inner resolve— with God's help— to rise to the challenges before him.

- Jay has not let the struggle against cancerous cells become a cancer upon his spirit. He finds ways to participate fully in life, God's precious gift to him. He has traveled widely, hunted, preached, and in many other venues shared his story of life and faith. And in all of the roller-coaster moments that typify the battle against childhood cancer, Jay has been good for a laugh!

- Jay wants to help people. He wants the meaning he has found in his experiences to be helpful and inspirational to others. And that's what his book is about. Not everyone who reads this book will know first-hand what it is like to live with cancer. And for this I thank God. But no one avoids pain and turmoil in life. So this book is for all of us, a reminder in times of trouble to look to the rock from which we are hewn.

When the Apostle Paul wrote to his friends at the church at Philippi, he said, "I thank my God for you every time I think of you; and every time I pray for you all, I pray with joy because of the way in which you have helped me in the work of the gospel from the very first day until now." That's how it is for me. I thank God for Jay every time I think of him. And I pray with joy every time I pray for him. And, yes, I think it is fair to say that from the very first day until now, Jay has helped me as I have sought to do the work of the gospel at a pediatric cancer center. Thank you, Jay!

David Mark Brown, M.Div.
Chaplain
St. Jude Children's Research Center

One of the pleasures of my life has been to meet and be associated with Jay Rogers. He has given so much to me in the years I have known him. The power and impact of his life are easily seen as one recognizes the character and zeal for life Jay has demonstrated. He has shown us that extreme difficulty in life can make us better and not bitter. His desire to write this book about his life experience and include in the book sermon outlines that will help anyone faced with life as he has been will benefit anyone wise enough to read it.

Jay loves sports and has drawn from that love a sense of dedication and work ethic that helps him face life every day. Like any good athlete, he knows that hard work and perseverance will pay off. He fights daily to do the best he can with the opportunities God has placed before him. It is with this sense of dedication and work that Jay has "fought the good fight" and has "run with patience the race that is set before him." Most impressively during his fight and the running of the race, he has kept his eye on Jesus, the one who makes the victory in his fight and race possible.

I have been inspired by this courageous young man who lives with such great hope, not just in this world but especially in the world to come. I do not know all that the book will contain at its conclusion, but I do know the one who is putting the book together. This knowledge makes it very easy to recommend this book and especially commend the life of its author as a great example for all of us to imitate. May God bless this young man and this book to be of great honor and glory to both God and to my very special friend, Jay.

Roy Sharp
Freed-Hardeman University
Henderson, Tennessee

It has been my privilege to have known Jay Rogers for four years. It was not until July 2010, that I became more acquainted with him. It was at that time that Tim, Wendy, Daniel, and Jay decided that they would work and worship with the Pleasant Hill church of Christ where I labor and worship. Since that time I have found Jay to be a great example of faithfulness. On one occasion a member of the congregation here stated that "Jay is a great example of what we all should be." I could not agree more. When I think of Jay, I am reminded of what a Christian is supposed to be! Jay is a Christian who is:

Courageous! "Only be thou strong and very courageous, that thou mayest observe to do according to all the law, which Moses my servant commanded thee: turn not from it to the right hand or to the left, that thou mayest prosper whithersoever thou goest" (Joshua 1:7). He, like Joshua, has courageously obeyed the Lord and preached the soul-saving Gospel of Christ. This courage has carried over into his battle with Ewing Sarcoma since November 2005.

Happy! Solomon, the wise man of old, said, "A merry heart doeth good like a medicine: but a broken spirit drieth the bones" (Proverbs 17:22). Jay always has a smile on his face. On one occasion my wife visited Jay in St. Jude and she commented afterward that he was still smiling even while receiving treatment. His attitude of happiness through adversity is a characteristic that all Christians should have.

Redeemed! On December 16, 2001, he was baptized into Christ by his father Tim. He heard the word of God which produces faith (Romans 10:17). He believed that Jesus Christ is the Son of God (John 3:16; 8:24). He repented of sins (Luke 13:3, 5; 2 Peter 3:9; Acts 2:38; 17:30). He confessed his faith in Christ (Matthew 10:32; Romans 10:9-10; Acts 8:37). And was baptized into Christ (Acts 2:38; Galatians 3:27; 1 Peter 3:21). Having done that, he has lived faithfully looking for that crown of life that our Heavenly Father will give at the last great day (Revelation 2:10; James 1:12).

Instant! Jay has been instant in his preaching the Gospel. Paul told young Timothy; "Preach the word; be instant in season, out of season; reprove, rebuke, exhort with all longsuffering and doctrine" (2 Timothy 4:2). Jay has preached when people desire to hear to the truth and even when maybe they did not. There may be some who will read this book who are not interested in spiritual things, but he has not shunned to proclaim the Gospel. He has been instant in preaching even when his health has not been what he desired it to be.

Serving The Lord! Since the Rogers' family has been worshipping with the Pleasant Hill congregation, Jay has used every opportunity to serve God. On one occasion Jay remarked, "I cannot do much, but I will do what I can." One area in which Jay is serving God is through sending cards. Jay sends cards to the sick, the bereaved, those who are celebrating birthdays or anniversaries, and those who just need a little bit of encouragement as Jay would say. He has used the ability to encourage others in serving the Lord. He is always ready to lead a prayer, and assist in teaching the teenagers in our Bible school program. He is "always abounding in the work of the Lord" for he knows that his "labor is not in vain in the Lord" (1 Corinthians 15:58).

Teaching Others The Gospel! "And Jesus came and spake unto them, saying, All power is given unto me in heaven and in earth. Go ye therefore, and teach all nations, baptizing them in the name of the Father, and of the Son, and of the Holy Ghost: Teaching them to observe all things whatsoever I have commanded you: and, lo, I am with you alway, even unto the end of the world. Amen" (Matthew 28:18-20). Jay is not physically able to go many places to teach others the Gospel but only eternity will show the good that will come from the publication of this book. A missionary was recently encouraged by him when he was preparing to go a campaign to Costa Rica when he received a check from Jay to help spread the Gospel. His helping finance that trip saw ten (10) precious souls obey the Gospel by being baptized into Christ.

Impact! Jay has had an impact on those around about him. He is like salt of which Jesus spoke; "Ye are the salt of the earth: but if the salt have lost his savour, wherewith shall it be salted? it is thenceforth good for nothing, but to be cast out, and to be trodden under foot of men" (Matthew 5:13). Jay had an impact on the staff at St. Jude Children's Research Hospital. He was telling me recently that one particular nurse always asks for Jay to be her patient. No doubt those things discussed already have had impact on this nurse. He had an impact on West Carroll High School where he attended school. That "never give up" attitude inspired members of the football team of which Jay was a member to not give up. Due to his impact on the school and especially the football team, his jersey was retired before he graduated high school. In the short time that his family has been at Pleasant Hill church of Christ he has had an impact on the congregation here. He has encouraged others to serve Christ, and one another. This book will have an impact on all who read it.

Anchored! Jay is anchored in Christ. His hope is in Christ and because of that he is not concerned about those things which are behind and he is pressing forward looking for that reward which is to come (cf. Hebrews 6:19; Philippians 3:13-16; Revelation 2:10; etc.). He is anchored in the Word of God. He is a student of the scriptures, searching them so that he will know the will of God (2 Timothy 2:15; 3:16-17; Philippians 1:7).

Name! Jay has a good family name. He is known because of the faithfulness and goodness of Tim and Wendy. They reared him well and he has followed that teaching. Note what Solomon said, "A good name is rather to be chosen than great riches, and loving favour rather than silver and gold" (Proverbs 22:1). When I first met Tim several years ago, he said he was "Jay's father." I believe that indicates that good name that Jay has chosen to have rather than so many other things such as gold and silver, and great riches. Also, Jay has chosen to wear the name, Christian, because he is following Christ (1 Corinthians 11:1)

It is without reservation that I commend to you, Jay Rogers! The Pleasant Hill church of Christ loves Tim, Wendy, Daniel, and Jay Rogers. Only eternity will show the good that will come from the efforts of Jay. Pray for Jay and his family during this time.

Jeff Brown
Pleasant Hill church of Christ
Trenton, Tennessee

23413151R00100

Made in the USA
Lexington, KY
13 June 2013